HOW TO WIN FRIENDS AND MANIPULATE PEOPLE

GEORGE MLADENOV

HarperCollinsPublishers

George Mladenov is a political operative from Bankstown in South-West Sydney and known best as 'King George of Bankstown'. He is widely regarded for captivating audiences through his shrewd negotiating style and strategic prowess in two seasons of the television show *Australian Survivor*, and later on *The Amazing Race Australia*. Before appearing on *Survivor*, George worked in public policy for a decade, both as the president of the Bankstown Labor Party as well as the chief policy advisor to a NSW Shadow Minister.

George's unique mindset has been moulded by three key things: a strong sense of community from his upbringing in a Macedonian-Greek household in Western Sydney; an innate ability to predict human behaviour after grinding out a living as a professional poker player; and a unique talent for getting his way through strategic influence learned from his political career.

HarperCollins*Publishers*
Australia • Brazil • Canada • France • Germany • Holland • India
Italy • Japan • Mexico • New Zealand • Poland • Spain • Sweden
Switzerland • United Kingdom • United States of America

HarperCollins acknowledges the Traditional Custodians
of the land upon which we live and work, and pays respect
to Elders past and present.

First published on Gadigal Country in Australia in 2023
by HarperCollins*Publishers* Australia Pty Limited
ABN 36 009 913 517
harpercollins.com.au

A catalogue record for this book is available from the National Library of Australia

ISBN 978 1 4607 6490 9 (paperback)
ISBN 978 1 4607 1684 7 (ebook)
ISBN 978 1 4607 3540 4 (audiobook)

Cover and internal design by Hazel Lam, HarperCollins Design Studio
Cover illustration copyright © Nigel Buchanan 2023
Typeset in Baskerville by Kelli Lonergan

Printed and bound by CPI Group (UK) Ltd, Croydon, CR0 4YY

To my parents, Kris and Maria, cleaners who sacrificed their own well-being to ensure that their children could be afforded the opportunities that they didn't have in life; and to the fantastic community of Bankstown, where winning friends and manipulating people just comes naturally because of who we are and where we are from.

CONTENTS

Introduction   1

PART 1 – WINNING FRIENDS
GATHERING YOUR LEGION OF DEVOTED FOLLOWERS

1   Believe in yourself and others will, too   15

2   Look after your own   51

3   Build a team of loyal allies   67

4   Win friends – and empty their wallets   84

5   Use criticism as an opportunity   100

6   Figure out what people want – then give it to them   124

7   Get out of your comfort zone   135

PART 2 – MANIPULATING PEOPLE
GETTING YOUR FRIENDS TO BEND TO YOUR WILL

8   Bend but don't break the rules   153

9   Get your way by helping other people get theirs   166

10 There is nothing better than a well-placed threat   175

11 Keep your closet free of skeletons   189

12 Manipulate a bad boss – and be a good one   202

13   Use stereotypes to your advantage   214

14   Gather information before you even need it   221

15   Watch how your enemies celebrate their wins   228

PART 3 – GLORY OR DEATH
WHAT TO DO WITH YOUR THRONE ONCE YOU HAVE TAKEN IT

16   Celebrate your own wins   247

17   When life gives you lemonade, package it and sell it 261

18   Know when to relinquish your power   274

19   Fight fire with fire   278

20   Use all of these tools to rule like a glorious king 283

Acknowledgments   310

INTRODUCTION

So far in my life, I've worked in politics as a trusted advisor, honed my instincts as a poker player, and appeared on some of the toughest reality-TV shows as a main character – three times. There's a common thread to succeeding in all of these fields: controlling situations, controlling outcomes and controlling people.

There is no doubt in my mind that you can succeed in both the personal and professional aspects of your life when you know how to effectively win friends and manipulate people. If you can nail this, like I have, you will get the outcome that you want in any situation.

And trust me, you *do* have those abilities – you just need to know how to bring them to the fore. That's what this book is for: teaching you the strategies I've learnt over my life for seizing power, but doing so with a smile that earns you legions of loyal followers.

You've probably bought this book because you know me as 'King George of Bankstown', the wily, villainous-when-it-counts, two-time *Australian Survivor* player and commentator, and contestant on *The Amazing Race Australia*. I'm here to tell you how I took that throne, and how you can seize power in your own suburbs. Follow my tips and you can be the hero and the villain at the same time.

The key to controlling situations is being able to play the hand that you have been dealt better than the people around you. As any good poker player will tell you, sometimes the cards in front of you don't matter – what is more important is how you play your opponent.

The ace up my sleeve is being from Bankstown. Having been born into this hustling Western Sydney suburb is what defines and has refined me. It is incredibly diverse and multicultural: Macedonian, Greek, Italian, Vietnamese and Lebanese cultures have framed the mindset and mentality of the locals. But Bankstown has its own identity, culture and a people who are fiercely proud of who they are and where they are from. Call us the Bravehearts of Australia: a nation within a nation of decent people who tell it like it is and deal with the consequences later.

Growing up in Bankstown has taught me a lot, but more than anything, it has given me the keys to be able to win friends and manipulate people – at the same time. You don't have to be the smartest person in the room to make mates and have them do your bidding, but you do need cunning, street smarts and confidence in your abilities.

You'll hear stories from my life – from my wily beginnings as a teenage poker champ, to the down and dirty backroom deals of politics, to the challenges of surviving one more day on *Survivor* and dashing around the world on *The Amazing Race*. You'll learn about my upbringing in working-class Bankstown as a twin son of two salt-of-the-earth parents who worked as cleaners all their lives to provide a better foundation for mine. I'll give you more than a few tips about why I was able to succeed as a character on reality TV, what I learned from the whole experience and show you how I manipulated my tribemates to become one of the most popular, prolific players in *Survivor* history. You'll learn how I was able to get there in the first place (and how you can, too) and had my fellow players hanging off my every word.

YOU DON'T HAVE TO BE THE SMARTEST PERSON IN THE ROOM TO MAKE MATES AND HAVE THEM DO YOUR BIDDING.

But as well as learning about me, I hope this book helps you learn about *you*. I aspire to help you achieve whatever it is you want in life and to be the best version of yourself you can be. I want you to have the confidence to make the right tactical decision to get the best outcome each and every time.

Whether it is in a family setting, workplace, sporting club, community group or religious hall, you will come across difficult people who stand in your way in every single facet of life – human obstacles who tend to overcomplicate things or unnecessarily obstruct the path forward. Often, these are the very people you need to befriend or work with to achieve your goals, even if you find the people torturous.

One of my favourite lines on this subject comes from football manager Bill Shankly: 'Football is a simple game complicated by idiots.' The same can be said of many other areas of life. (Except *Survivor*, that is: *Survivor* is a complex game complicated by idiots. That's why it's so difficult to play for most people and so entertaining to watch for audiences across the world.) But the real life of jobs, relationships, families, friends? That's also a simple game complicated by idiots.

Sure, you can navigate through life avoiding the idiots. But – spoiler alert – they're everywhere. From the instant you leave your house in the morning to the moment you return home at night, you'll bump into idiots. (And, if you're unlucky, they live inside your house, too.)

You can't avoid them. In fact, to get ahead you *need* them. So it's far better to learn some simple tricks to manipulate the difficult people standing in your way and get to your desired outcome quickly, with as few bridges burned as possible.

Now, I'm not a nihilist. I don't think every last person on earth except me (and *you*, obviously – you bought this book, you're clearly one of the good ones) is an idiot. Connections are important: with friends, family members, loved ones and co-workers. No-one is an island, and good allies are critical in life.

Learning how to get what you want is taboo to many people. It's one thing to manipulate the idiots in your life, but manipulating your friends and loved ones? That would make you a villain!

But not all villains are evil. Some people who go on reality-TV shows struggle with being perceived as a villain, but if you can be a *lovable* villain then you can win the hearts of the public without losing face.

In other words, you can be like me.

People love to watch *Survivor* for this very reason. Despite the fact the contestants are placed in hostile locations and improbable circumstances, the show really is a reflection of the world we live in and the situations we navigate in everyday life. In this way, *Survivor* is a lot like my previous career in politics. There are two sides to every argument and often multiple factions within a tribe. Both are high-pressure games where you have to outwit, outplay and outlast your opponents to win the hearts and minds of those around you.

There's a reason I burst onto *Survivor* as a first-time player but battled like a fully evolved version of myself and dominated the beginners. I was able to pull off big moves that left my opponents wondering how I was always two steps ahead. It was a sneakiness, a cunning I'd honed during my years as a political operative, making things happen within the shadowy underbelly of the governmental process.

In life, as in politics, there are always levers you can pull and key choices you can make to get the outcome that you need. The key is being able to understand the perspective of the person you need to influence. If you can do this, you will win friends as well as win the game, generating the ultimate win–win situation. It's positive manipulation.

IF YOU CAN ADDRESS THE MOTIVATIONS AND PRIORITIES OF THOSE AROUND YOU WHILE STILL GETTING WHAT YOU WANT, THEN YOU CAN STEP INTO THE ROLE OF THE LOVABLE VILLAIN.

And every villain needs their prince or princess – the light to their darkness, the sun to their shadow. This duality is vital, as it's important to surround yourself with people who think differently to you. When I had the chance to go on *The Amazing Race Australia*, I chose my sister Pam as my teammate because great things can happen when you are able to see things from an alternative perspective. Pam is nine years younger than me, a hairdresser, and someone who rides her emotions visibly and publicly – not like me. On a poker table, she'd be the kind of player I'd deliberately target for easy chips when things don't go her way.

Everybody has a Pam in their life and family: the polar opposite to you, but tied by blood. The hardest thing in working with family members is managing a forever relationship when there are competing interests. But if you can truly master the art of compromise – which you will after

WINNING FRIENDS AND
MANIPULATING PEOPLE ARE
NOT MUTUALLY EXCLUSIVE;
WHAT BENEFITS YOU
CAN ALSO BENEFIT OTHERS.

reading this book – you can win the favour of your family to positively manipulate a situation for yourself. It's less work in the long run to have them do your bidding, and it also makes for more enjoyable dinner-table conversations.

Like my other passion, football, there are many different strategies you can employ to navigate the game of life. You can play an attacking game or a defensive game. You can apply pressure at certain times while absorbing it at others. You can be in complete control, let your guard down and then get blindsided by others when you least expect it, or you can play a passive game and scrape your way to the end by holding on for dear life and hoping some luck comes your way.

Most importantly, in *Survivor* and in life, if you find your tribe, your people, no matter what the setting, be loyal to them and keep them on your side. Work out what they want and what you need, and find a way to make everyone happy. Winning friends and manipulating people are not mutually exclusive; what benefits you can also benefit others.

Now, some people might bristle at having the concepts of 'friendship' and 'manipulation' sit so closely together. To them I would say: the outcome is more important than the interpretation. If you can operate successfully as both a friend and manipulator without your manipulatee knowing the difference, then it doesn't really matter.

Through this book, I will give you all the weapons you need in your arsenal to subtly take control of any situation and achieve your desired outcome. I will teach you not to think of manipulation as a dirty word: to confidently use it as a means of attack or defence, no matter what the setting.

By the time you've finished reading this book, you will know how to play your cards correctly, to navigate the obstacles and win at the simple game of life. If you follow my advice, you will find yourself surrounded by loyal devotees who will do anything for you.

To the rest, I say this: glory or death!

PART 1

WINNING FRIENDS

GATHERING YOUR LEGION OF DEVOTED FOLLOWERS

CHAPTER 1

BELIEVE IN YOURSELF AND OTHERS WILL, TOO

Throughout my life on the throne, I have mined every experience for gems to place in my crown. I have learned to be strategic, pragmatic, mathematical, logical and to think on my feet. I have perfected how to keep circumstance and luck on my side, and how to banish the naysayers who stand in my way. But as I've realised, the most important attribute to have if you want to rule is self-belief. If you don't believe in yourself as a leader, why should anybody else?

This is never more true than when you are auditioning to be beamed into hundreds of thousands of homes, three nights a week, for months on end.

As I navigated this process trying to get onto my first *Survivor* season in 2019, I was hiding a dirty little secret: 10 years earlier, I'd utterly flopped my first reality-TV audition. It was a failure that haunted me for years, one that I was terrified I might repeat.

The difference in the two outcomes all came down to one of the most important qualities you can bring to any situation, whether it's an audition or a job interview, a first date or a wedding speech: confidence. It sounds so simple, right? But for most people, it's not. It certainly wasn't for me, all those years ago. So many of us can project an air of assurance when we're at home alone, only to flounder when it really matters and the pressure is on. I know, because I used to be like that, too.

'King George of Bankstown' arrived on your screens in 2021 fully formed, but before that, he took some work. If you told me at my *Amazing Race*–themed 16th birthday party that I would play *Survivor* twice, be called one of the worldwide greats, and then go on *The Amazing Race* as a *Survivor* legend, I would have never believed it in a million years.

That's because before I created the Kingdom to live my best life in I had to spend a good 10 years striving to reach the level of self-belief needed to confidently wear the crown in the first place. At 16 I had lots of dreams and ambition, but I was also riddled with self-doubt and saddled with an unhealthy obsession with reality-TV shows.

I grew up hooked on reality TV. I loved two shows in particular: *Survivor* and *The Amazing Race* (and no, I'm not just saying that because they're two I've been on).

That's the first step to making it on reality TV: watch a lot of it. How can you expect to succeed if you're not a student of the genre? Watch as much as you can, and learn what works – which personalities, which moves, which storylines.

I watched the US *Survivor* from the first season, when Richard Hatch – the OG *Survivor* villain! – sat around naked at camp, annoyed just about all of his tribemates and somehow still managed to walk away with the million-dollar prize.

I thought he was great (although his lack of attire wasn't my cup of tea). I have always loved the dastardly, scheming players – the Sandras, the Jonny Fairplays. They're the players you remember, right? The ones who seem like they were waiting their whole lives to play the game; the ones who revel in the dirtiness of it.

I was such a fan as a teenager, I even had one whole area of my bedroom filled with VHS tapes (remember those?) full of the first few seasons of *Survivor* and *The Amazing Race*, so I could rewatch them to my heart's content. Once technology got a little better, I'd be up at 5am every day to download the latest episode of US *Survivor* that had aired overnight and watch it before school.

I even used to play online *Survivor* games. The hardcore fans of the show will know what I'm talking about (and if so, I may have even played with you back in the day). *Survivor* fans around the world run their own online-only version of the game – called Orgs – complete with immunity challenges, tribal councils and plenty of instant-messaging scandal. The games run over several weeks, just like the real *Survivor*, where you form alliances, build résumés and vote out your peers, one by one.

While nothing can really compare to being on a beach in Samoa or in the dust of the Australian Outback, these games can still test your mettle when it comes to things like building alliances and showing your endurance … even if you are behind a computer screen the whole time. They're still popular among the more committed members of the *Survivor* fanbase, particularly in the US.

I spent a lot of time as a teenager shut away in my room playing online *Survivor*; I was as dedicated back then as I am now. I particularly remember one challenge that required a player from each tribe to post one 'fire' emoji every minute. The team who lasted the longest would be declared the winner.

I was on the bottom of my tribe and the last surviving member of my alliance. I knew I had to do whatever it took to make sure my tribe won the challenge, or else I'd be voted out. I was committed to the game and wanted to make it to the merge, which was going to be soon, so I took on the full weight of the task on behalf of my team and dedicated myself to posting a fire emoji every minute.

I was committed. So bloody committed, in fact, that I posted an emoji on the minute, every minute, for 17 and a half hours. I realised within the first hour that I was the only person in my tribe of four that was contributing to the challenge. I knew I was likely doomed – I figured the other three were not participating because they wanted to lose so they could vote me out – but that was also why I *had* to keep posting that fire emoji each and every minute, to win immunity and stay in the game.

But I also had to stay in school. This was before the days of smartphones, so I parked myself at the library computer, skipping my classes to keep posting. The librarian didn't question me; I was the top student and seemingly 'studying' as I was constantly typing. When school was done for the day, I continued to post into the night, with my mum kindly bringing me food and water, and my few toilet breaks had to be done within 60 seconds.

And guess what? After 17 and a half hours, my tribe still didn't win. I went to bed in the middle of the night after pulling what I thought was enough of a lead on the other two tribes – who both had *all* of their players posting, distributing the workload – but eventually, I relented. I woke up after a few hours' sleep to see that the challenge had ended. My tribe had finished last, and we were going to tribal council.

I had failed, and they voted me out pretty quickly after that. They had successfully thrown the challenge and I didn't make it to merge. To think of all the effort I had gone through! And it was all for nothing.

This taught me a valuable lesson I'd eventually take with me into my two real-life *Survivor* seasons: work smarter, not harder. Instead of putting 17 and a half hours towards smashing a keyboard, I could have spent that time building better relationships. I could've spent time convincing people that to work with me was in their best interest further on in the game. The only thing that matters in the game of *Survivor* (and in politics) is making sure you have the numbers –

and the friends – to back you up when you are in trouble. If I had spent more energy earlier on in the game forming better friendships, I could've been in the alliance that controlled the tribe rather than the sole remaining member of the minority that kept being voted off. I needed to make an impression through relationships and strategy, not in my determination to perform in the challenges. If I had played smarter, it would have been less energy-intensive and handed me a more lucrative outcome. From that moment onward, I was much more careful about which path I chose.

After years of watching reality TV and playing *Survivor* games online, I figured it was time for the real thing. My first proper brush with the cameras came when I was 21, for the second season of *The Amazing Race Australia*. My twin brother, Steve, and I, already big fans of the show, auditioned together. We'd even worked out a golden television hook to make us stand out: we're twins – but we're opposite twins rather than identical ones. Sure, we did everything together growing up: same clothes (thanks, Mum), same school (but never in the same class), same soccer team. But despite this, we are the opposites of each other and not super close.

Everything you need to know about Steve took place in the womb before we were even born. We were actually meant to be triplets – there were three of us in there. But then our poor other brother/sister died in utero at around four months old. I always ponder on whether I absorbed that almost-sibling's personality, giving me extra.

More problems hit at the seven-month mark of the pregnancy. Steve was not in the best shape and we both had to exit our mother eight weeks early. (I have no doubt in my mind that I would've grown to be a 200-centimetre Adonis if we'd stayed in the womb for those extra eight weeks.)

So out we came. I emerged surprisingly energetic and healthy. Steve, sick and weak, went straight into an incubator for a month. Doctors searched in vain for a personality, but tragically it appears he was born without one. He was otherwise healthy and normal.

I like joking about my twin brother. He's actually OK, but we don't have an awful lot in common beyond having shared a womb for seven months, and a love of adventure-based reality-TV shows all our lives.

Which is how we ended up auditioning for *The Amazing Race* together as 21-year-olds. The chalk-and-cheese-twins angle stood out to the executives. Even at 21, I was already thinking like a good casting producer and making the job of pitching an angle easy for them.

During one interview, Steve sat there silently next to me while I badgered him to talk. 'Come on, Steve, say something interesting!' I jibed. 'At least pretend you have a personality!'

The *Amazing Race* producers *did* think this sounded like great TV, and we were summoned to a hotel in Sydney for a final interview with the head honchos of the show. We had even pre-filled a number of visa forms. It was incredibly exciting!

I don't know what we were expecting – I don't think we even *thought* about what to expect, we were so young. But there is one thing that I definitely didn't have then: confidence.

By the time we walked into that interview, we were really feeling the nerves. There, in a hotel room cleared of most of its furniture, sat a row of intimidating-looking TV types, perched behind a table and ready to grill us.

It was like a funeral home in there, the entire room covered in white sheets. There was no vibe – we were expecting a super-casual chat, not a formal, straight-faced evaluation. I was so naive that when I learned we'd be meeting in a hotel room, I thought we would all be sitting around on a bed together! Instead, we were treated like performing monkeys, summoned to put on a show from scratch. But we were too green to figure that out straight away, so instead we matched our energy to the people interviewing us: open-casket-level energy with an added bit of jitters.

I could feel my brother shrinking away inside himself – and I could feel it happening to me, too. My voice barely came out as a squeak; all the big game I assumed I'd talk just didn't come. The interview was excruciating. Within minutes of sitting down, I knew that we'd both blown it.

It was a complete disaster. When they asked Steve about himself, he responded: 'I'm Steve.' I remember talking about my want for adventure and not our relationship. I was shaking from nerves and after about five minutes they frogmarched us out of that hotel room.

Steve and I sat on the train back to Bankstown in silence, defeated. We didn't say a word to each other between Kings Cross and Sydenham stations. This was meant to be the best thing we would ever do in our lives together and we had fallen at the first major hurdle: the need to promote ourselves and our story to the people in control of our destinies.

Unfortunately, a bad audition is not like a bad job interview – you can't just get on with your life without having some painful reminders of your defeat. A few months later, the season aired, and there on screen was a team with the same gimmick as us: two chalk-and-cheese siblings from

Western Sydney. I'll never forget their names: Joey and Grace. I watched the whole season with envy coursing through my veins every time they were on screen. They were no George and Steve … but then, I guess they didn't bomb the audition.

Almost a decade later, I still had my failed audition filed away in the back of my head: one of those 'ya blew it' private humiliations that came flooding back in moments of self-recrimination. I knew I'd still be cringing about on my deathbed. If only I could get another chance, I thought, I'd nail it this time, and correct all my mistakes.

And then, in December of 2019, I saw an ad on TV calling for auditions for the next season of *Australian Survivor*, filming a few months later in 2020 (or so they thought).

Something clicked. This is it, I thought. Now or never!

So I tried to film an audition tape. I recorded the first take in the exact space where I'd filmed the *Amazing Race* video with Steve nine years before: our downstairs living room, '80s brown carpet out of frame, camera on the dining table. Like that first audition, it was a bit of a disaster. Video editing is not my forte, so I knew I had no choice but to keep it simple, just talking into my smartphone screen. But as soon as I'd hit record, the old problem from that first attempt reared its head again.

I knew my story would be interesting – a Labor branch executive from the Western suburbs who would play a big, never-seen-before game. I had the right message, but as I tried to record the video in the swim trunks I would eventually wear onto the show, I struggled to express myself and my story. I watched my attempted video back on my phone and felt the weight from that failed *Amazing Race* interview press down on me, smothering me.

After a few aborted takes at filming something better, I put the whole endeavour into the too-hard basket. I convinced myself that I didn't need to apply for *Survivor*; I had a great work–life balance at the time, having moved from politics to a mentally unstimulating job in government policy. But still, something niggled away at me. I hadn't quite given up. I knew I could be an incredible player.

A month later, I was out in Sydney on a pub crawl with my two good mates Mike and Stevie. Mike's a hilarious German with a strong accent; Stevie is a fun but quiet Sri Lankan–Australian who balances out our friend circle.

I like to look after my closest friends on a night out, so settling in at an exclusive cocktail bar in Sydney's Circular Quay, I perused the menu and announced, 'I'll have three million-dollar martinis, please.'

Mike looked at his menu, and his jaw fell open. 'Nein, George, why on earth are you ordering *that*?'

While the martinis weren't actually a million dollars, they *were* $250 each. That's a good 25 vodka Red Bulls down at Bankstown Sports Club.

'Because I want to,' I told him. I'd recently had a big win at a poker tournament, so I had money to blow, and I wanted to treat my friends to something extravagant. Looking back on it now, I think I was feeling a little lost and embarrassed about my inability to put down a simple audition tape, and I wanted to talk about it – but with Mike and Stevie, who definitely did not watch *Survivor*. If I was going to ask for life advice on something they didn't know about, then I was going to make this round of drinks worth their while.

Out the martinis came, each on its own special little tray, trimmed with gold leaf, looking like an impulsive use of $750.

After a few sips of the most expensive drink I've ever had in my life, I turned to my friends. It was like I'd just drunk truth serum, like that lavish drink had given me permission to be truly vulnerable with them. Suddenly, it all came tumbling out.

I told them that I wanted to be a *Survivor* contestant. I'd be so good at it, I *knew* I would. I explained that I felt like

I'd been training for it all my life. But … I just couldn't get the first step of the process right: a short video that reflected who I was as a person. I wanted to apply for *Survivor*, but I looked like a lamb and not a lion on my video attempt.

Mike and Stevie were as supportive as you'd expect two friends who'd just been treated to $250 worth of cocktails each.

'Just be yourself!' they assured me. 'Be "pub-crawl George" – fun and confident!'

The three of us always enjoy our pub crawls on a Saturday night. We usually start at somewhere central and then venture off into the night getting to know different groups of people. New bar, new crowd, new story. None of us had an issue with confidence; you need it to walk up to people you don't know and end the night calling them a friend. But Mike and Stevie were right – for some reason that confidence dissolved as soon as I started to sell myself into my smartphone screen.

We continued the night – immediately reverting to much cheaper drinks – but their words stuck with me. Of course I can strike up a conversation with anyone in any circumstance. I have no problem getting to know people at local pubs and clubs; in fact, it's a good way to get to know what members of the local community are thinking.

I had done this all the time when I'd been a political staffer and needed to advise my boss. Want to know what different crowds think about a controversial political issue? Head down to the local RSL and ask them, whether they are the group of older Greek men studying the form guide or a hen's night gaggle draped in pink feather-boas and drinking through novelty straws.

I don't lack confidence in daily life, but I was lacking the self-belief to do well in another reality-TV audition. I just had to speak to my phone (and the TV executives who would be watching the video) as if they were a new friend I had just made down at the pub.

The next morning, I dragged my dusty self out of bed (Did you know you can still get a hangover from a $250 cocktail? Seems rude) and hopped behind the wheel of my horrible little Rio 2000 to do the only thing I had planned for the day: go to the physio for a massage. (Always use up your private health insurance benefits before the end of the calendar year!)

After my physio appointment was over, I remembered the advice Mike and Stevie had given me. Now or never, George. I pulled out my phone, started recording and spoke into the screen from the driver's seat of my car.

'Hi, my name is George Mladenov. I'm 30 years old, and I'm a political operative from Bankstown. I'm applying for *Survivor* because I think it's about time you had a *real* operator on your show – a political operator.'

With those two sentences, I immediately told the execs exactly who I was. But I didn't stop there.

'I mean, you've had a bunch of teachers, you've had a bunch of models, you've had a bunch of kids on there who think they know what they're doing. They think they know how to work a crowd, they think they know how to spin a yarn, but let me tell you – they don't have a clue.'

Where was this coming from? It was everything I'd told myself sitting in front of the TV, watching *Survivor* all these years. I delivered my story and message with the confidence and self-belief that it deserved – to the people in charge of casting the show. I'd unlocked my power. Pub-crawl George was unleashed.

I kept talking: I told them I was the president of the Labor Party in Bankstown, and I'd worked as a political staffer, a job that involved controlling and manipulating with lots of scheming and strategising. I told them I was Bankstown born and bred and what that means to me: I have immense pride for my hometown, and I'm never afraid to stand up for myself and tell it like it is.

It was all over in about 90 seconds. As I watched it back, I finally believed that I had done a good job, but thought I needed a little bit more to pique some interest. I'd shaken off the nerves and told my story in a way that packed a punch. And I'd done it in a single take.

Upstairs on my bed later that morning, eating my hangover KFC (See, KFC? I really do love you – I'm ready for that endorsement deal whenever you are), I felt I needed to give them a little something more and to add some humour into the mix.

I took off my shirt, lay back down on my bed and pressed record. Bear in mind, I was still around 90kg then – this was before I did a hasty pre-television F45 boot camp. The camera didn't exactly love me, but hey, I loved myself.

'Well, here I am again,' I announced, my bare shoulders and chest in shot. 'I figured you need to see a bit of skin, because you're gonna see some skin on the island.'

And then my dog Douglas – then just a three-year-old puppy – jumped on the bed and started licking the chicken grease off my face. I thought this showed my softer side as a dog daddy, so I kept recording. As Douglas busied himself

French-kissing every inch of my face, I finished with an ultimatum.

'So, do you want an interesting season? Pick me. If you don't want an interesting season, don't pick me.' I shrugged, trying my best to play hard-to-get while Douglas licked chicken crumbs off my fingers. 'I'll run for council instead. The pre-selection will be on when *Survivor* is filming. So I'll either be on *Survivor*, or the next mayor of Bankstown!'

And that was it. No big gimmicks, no flashy settings, just me, telling them what I'd bring to the table. But I had added those vital ingredients that had been missing for so long: confidence and self-belief.

Here's some crucial advice, for those reading this and wondering how to 'get' confidence. Whether you actually *have* confidence or you're just faking it for the moment, it doesn't matter to the outside observer. They can't tell the difference. They don't know you're bricking it inside. And here's the other secret: faked confidence does, more often than not, quickly turn into earned confidence. You can even trick yourself! And if you believe in yourself, I can guarantee you others will.

The casting producers didn't know about my first failed video attempts or that I had once bombed an *Amazing Race*

WHETHER YOU ACTUALLY *HAVE* CONFIDENCE OR YOU'RE JUST FAKING IT FOR THE MOMENT, IT DOESN'T MATTER TO THE OUTSIDE OBSERVER. THEY CAN'T TELL THE DIFFERENCE.

audition. They saw a confident person, heard an interesting story and that was enough.

I quickly progressed to the next stage: a Skype interview. I was still working at the NSW Health Ministry at the time, and popping into a meeting room for an hour to chat to a reality-TV producer about escaping your humdrum office existence is generally frowned on in most workplaces. So I booked a meeting room for my scheduled call and labelled it something vague, important-sounding and serious, so people would know I was busy and wouldn't be tempted to drop in. In this case it was a 'palliative-care stakeholder meeting'.

I tried to relax with the woman on the call – but I was also worried about being sprung by one of my bosses at work.

'If I give the signal,' I asked her, 'can you ask me to read you the minutes from the last end-of-life internal conference? Or tell me we need to start thinking about next year's budgets?'

Rather than being annoyed, she seemed quite tickled by the request. Here I was, in my *Survivor* pre-interview, forming an alliance with the interviewer and getting her on board with my sneaky scheme. I was made for this.

Our palliative-care stakeholder meeting went for a good 45 minutes. I told her I was a massive *Survivor* fan, but that wasn't the focus – she was far more interested in my political background and how I'd bring that acumen to the show. I expanded on my audition tape, explaining all the ways a job in the dark backrooms of politics would be the perfect preparation for wheeling and dealing on the show.

A few weeks went by, and I got a call to come to a hotel in Surry Hills for an in-person audition. Memories of my old *Amazing Race* flop came flooding back, and those old nerves set in again.

It was the words of another friend who set me right. During a coffee break the day before the audition, with my designated work-wife, Jess Hresc, I admitted to her what I was doing and that I was nervous I was going to stuff it up again. (Like any good public servant, I would regularly try to lift staff morale and productivity by going on coffee breaks.)

'Jess, I can't screw this up,' I said. 'I just want to show them who I am, but I always get nervous at job interviews. And I *bombed* the last time I was in a situation like this.'

'Just be Saturday-night George!' was her advice, so similar to Mike's.

I may have taken her advice a little too literally. On the morning of the audition, I noticed there was an open pub across the road from the hotel where the audition was taking place. On an impulse, I slipped in and ordered myself a triple vodka Red Bull. Saturday-night George, activated.

Survivor auditions are a funny beast. Because the whole show is about working in a group, you audition in a pack, not solo. Unlike my *Amazing Race* try-out with my brother, where it was just us in the room because it would just be us on the road, I was thrust together with a bunch of other hopefuls and we all auditioned together. The producers needed to test our interpersonal skills to see who could make friends (or enemies) quickly, and who became part of the hotel wallpaper.

My group was an eclectic bunch of around 30. There were the usual super-fit *Survivor* types and some real high achievers; one man was both impossibly handsome and a doctor, surely a good candidate for *The Bachelor* if *Survivor* knocked him back.

Then there were some more … *colourful* people. One girl was *all* colour, with tie-dyed clothes, vivid tattoos and rainbow dreadlocks. I kept forgetting her name because I called her 'the circus lady' in my head. (Circus lady, if you're reading this, I'm sorry. Please book me on Cameo and I'll apologise personally.)

I, on the other hand, wore a white T-shirt, white shorts and white loafers. I know that sounds like I'd dressed up in a costume, but I was just wearing what I thought looked good –

what I'd bought from Bankstown Square to wear for a night on the town.

AS IT TURNS OUT, DRESSING LIKE YOU'RE IN A NAPISAN COMMERCIAL IMMEDIATELY MAKES YOU STAND OUT IN A GROUP AUDITION.

We all stood in a horseshoe shape and went around the group to deliver a brief spiel about ourselves. I had one eye on anyone who might fit the same mould as me – someone who might fill my stereotype. I spotted him quickly: a lawyer with a Southern-European background from Western Sydney. As another person with a Southern-European background and a law degree from Western Sydney, this was definitely an alternate me. (I finished my law degree and was admitted by the Supreme Court of NSW at 26 – a sentence that cost me $60,000 in student debt). Luckily for me, his spiel was dull. I can beat him onto this show, I thought.

It was almost my turn to speak, and I was getting nervous. The man on my left announced his name, but I was so busy focusing on what I'd say next that I immediately forgot it.

Then he launched into an intense, legitimately inspiring story about how he'd managed to overcome adversity through the medium of judo.

I was only half listening though. I was furiously contemplating what I should say, when the producer conducting the audition yelled, 'Next!'

I took a deep breath.

'That was a very sad story, whatever your name is,' I stated. 'Hi everybody, my name is George Mladenov. I don't have a sad story, but I *am* the president of the Labor Party in Bankstown.'

It wasn't my most tactful moment, but people laughed, including the guy next to me. (I'm glad he found it funny – after all, he was a black belt.)

Pushing on, I told the room that I never missed an opportunity to canvass. I asked them all to vote for me at the next Canterbury–Bankstown Council election because if I didn't make it onto *Survivor*, I'd be running for Council. Again, people laughed. (I was being serious. I wanted – and still do – to deliver an improved quality of life for local residents by increasing access to local government services.) Two laughs, some interest – I figured I was making some friends. This was certainly going better than my last hotel-room audition.

When everyone had finished giving their spiel, it was time to answer another question: 'If you had to vote out one person right now, who would it be?'

The first person chose me. And the second. And the third. Around the horseshoe it went, with all but a couple of my new tribemates choosing me to be voted off the pretend island that was this inner-city hotel.

A few gave explanations, echoing the first person's half-hearted reasoning that I was too political. Brash. Not to be trusted.

Screw these arseholes, I thought initially. But then another thought occurred to me, one that made me grin from ear to ear: they all remembered me. In a group full of strangers, where we all struggled to remember the names of the people standing next to us — even the judo black belt and the hyper-coloured hundreds-and-thousands woman — I'd obviously made an impression.

When it came time for me to give my answer, I brushed off any hurt feelings and slapped that fake-it-until-you-make-it confident smile on my face.

I perused my traitorous tribemates with my eyes.

'Him,' I announced, pointing at the doctor at the front of the line. 'He's a hot doctor and everyone seems to love him, so he's not going to get a vote for a while. I want to get him out now while I can.'

People laughed. I was being serious.

As the audition continued, I continued to label the others as I saw them. The hot doctor. The boring lawyer. The circus lady. Sure, it was more than a bit rude, but these people had all just united to insist that I should be voted out. I was happy to make a few enemies – and show that their personalities could be boiled down to a few choice words.

It wasn't the most subtle of tactics, but I wanted the execs running the audition to see that these people were so unremarkable that I couldn't even remember their names. And it certainly rattled my hopeful future tribemates – they shot me annoyed looks every time I called them by their unflattering nicknames.

Next, we were split into two groups and had to compete in a fake immunity challenge (it involved stacking blocks – no mud pit or fire-making in this hotel room). I quietly formed an alliance with the circus lady as we prepared, sidling up to her and reasoning that we might lose the challenge, so we should stick together and vote out the hot doctor. She was down for that.

As predicted, our tribe lost, and we were sent to fake tribal council. It was a classic King George tribal council where I started on the bottom and came out on top. Looking back on it now, it was almost a dress rehearsal for situations that would later play out for me on the show: I was the target of an alliance trying to vote me out, so I won the trust of a bunch of underestimated women and convinced them (for an entirely made-up reason) to target someone else – in this case, it was the hot doctor.

The hot doctor was seated next to the only other person in the room who could've been a rival character to me. He was around my age, also from Western Sydney, and was the third lawyer in the room. (This may sound like overkill before you remember that they were casting for Brains v Brawn, even if we didn't know it at the time.) The only difference between us was that he looked ripped, with muscles bulging under his suit. Brains *and* brawn.

I didn't want to give this person a label, because I wanted to own the space to stand out as the brainy guy from Bankstown. So I kept asking for his name but would never use it to make him seem forgettable. I called him the unknown guy.

The unknown guy led the challenge with the hot doctor as well as the discussion to vote me out. It was a heated tribal; I kept seeking the support of the quiet women on my left, and in the end, after we voted, it was a tied vote between myself and the hot doctor! A big improvement from the near-unanimous vote against me one hour earlier in the horseshoe.

The group audition wrapped, and we were told that those who'd been successful could expect a call later that day inviting them back tomorrow. I felt very hopeful – it was the inverse of my audition-that-shall-not-be-named all those years ago: I'd made an impression. I'd made people laugh (albeit unintentionally). And above all, I'd stood out. Sure, all my new tribemates wanted to vote me out, but most of them were boring – King George wasn't!

My friends' advice, the roll I'd been on in my previous interviews, and the Dutch courage from my triple vodka Red Bull had all gelled together and I'd had no inhibitions at the audition. I'd absolutely slayed.

I jumped on the train back to Bankstown, my knees jiggling with anticipation below my white shorts. We were told not to speak to any other applicants, but the judo expert was in the same carriage as me. The temptation was intense, but despite our urges, we stuck to the rules, keeping to ourselves aside from sharing the occasional knowing glance.

While we were on the train, Mr Judo got the phone call to come to the final audition the next day. I could hear his end of the conversation and see the glee on his face. I was surprised and more than a little envious. *Him?* Really? After he hung up, he looked so pleased with himself – he wanted to celebrate, but we were forbidden to speak, so all we could really do was smile at each other. I held my phone, ready and waiting for my call. And waiting. And waiting.

As I got off at Bankstown, I broke my vow of silence with Mr Judo, figuring we'd never see each other again. It takes a long time to get back to my neighbourhood, and my phone still hadn't rung.

'Good luck, I hope you do well,' I said earnestly. 'It looks like I'm not getting the call.'

I walked back home from the station and was greeted by Mum, asking me how I thought I went. As I slunk upstairs, I told her that I thought I'd nailed it, but other people had already got the call. 'I think I'm out,' I admitted. I think Mum seemed relieved.

I plonked myself on the couch in our upstairs living room to ponder where it had all gone wrong. Had I gone too hard, been too brash, just been too 'me'? After about an hour of mindless phone scrolling, suddenly the words 'PRIVATE NUMBER' appeared on my phone. I almost dropped the damn thing as I rushed to answer.

'Hello, George speaking!' I said, clearly eager. If it was a telemarketer, I probably would have thrown my mobile out the window.

It wasn't. It was a member of the *Survivor* casting team. They wanted me back for the next round of auditions.

I couldn't say yes quickly enough! I screamed with delight knowing that the next round of auditions – the one-on-one interview with the production and television executives – was the final stage of the process. Friday 4pm would decide my destiny.

The first text I fired off was to my manager at work, advising that my food poisoning hadn't abated and I would need one more day of sick leave. I then texted Mike and Stevie, saying I was at the final stage with an interview in the city at 4pm, and that I would meet them for a pub crawl afterwards at 6pm.

The next morning, before I trekked it back into the city, I allowed some time to check in with myself. I knew I needed to give myself the sort of much-needed pep talk I'd lacked back when I was 21 and in the same situation.

Here's what I told myself: 'You have absolutely nothing to lose. Give it everything you've got, and you can worry about whether or not they liked it when you're on the train home later.'

BEING MYSELF IS WHAT HAD GOT ME HERE, NOT TRYING TO GAME THE SYSTEM OR GIVING THEM WHAT I *THOUGHT* THEY WANTED.

I was just being George, political operative from Bankstown. Pub-crawl George. Saturday-night George. That's what I was offering, and it was 100 per cent me. So far, they seemed to like it; they obviously liked me, my story and the kind of player I was offering to be. So that day I'd just keep doing what I was doing: be George.

Up I went in the hotel elevator. Was I feeling confident? Yes. I knew that I could deliver 'me', but the question was if that was what they were after. The stakes felt impossibly high, and I desperately didn't want to blow it.

The audition wasn't without its challenges. I might have left my self-doubt outside, but the casting team hadn't brought any enthusiasm inside, either. It was very similar to that disastrous *Amazing Race* audition all those years earlier:

a near-empty hotel room, a row of TV execs and a complete lack of vibe.

But this time, *I* brought the vibe. I was full of confidence (or at least the appearance of confidence) and felt truly in the moment. It was like I had just downed a second million-dollar martini and was about to call for another round.

It was clear they'd loved everything I'd offered in the audition process to date, and it was also clear they wanted me to lean even further into that element of my personality. I was happy to oblige, regaling them with stories about my days as a political operative and outlining my big plans for the show: scheme, backstab, manipulate. Control the numbers as a 'faceless man', which in political speak means the decisionmaker behind the scenes. All those juicy *Survivor* traits.

After a while, they told me they'd asked all of their planned questions – but still we kept talking. And talking. One producer asked me if I'd like to be Prime Minister one day.

I scoffed. 'Absolutely not. Why would I want to be the Prime Minister? If I ever get elected to parliament, and I am in majority government, I want to be the minister that controls what happens in the caucus room – because then I control the numbers, and then I can control the

CONTROL THE NUMBERS AS A 'FACELESS MAN', WHICH IN POLITICAL SPEAK MEANS THE DECISIONMAKER BEHIND THE SCENES.

other ministers. And when something goes wrong, I'm not the sacrificial lamb that gets sent to the wolves. I'll chop someone else's head off instead.'

They all looked a bit stunned. I kept going.

'That's exactly what I'm going to do on *Survivor*. I'm going to control the numbers. And when something goes wrong, someone else takes the blame, they go home and I'll make it to the end.'

By this point, they were all grinning from ear to ear. They laughed. I was being serious.

That night, I caught up as planned with Mike and Stevie for a drink on George Street in Sydney (not a pun, just the street). Only a couple of months earlier, I'd been pouring my heart out to them. Today, I had a very different, much happier story to report.

'Mike,' I admitted. 'I killed it. I think I'm going to be on *Survivor*.'

There were no million-dollar martinis on the menu, so three celebratory triple vodka Red Bulls would have to do.

A few weeks later, after picking up every unknown number on the first ring, I got the call.

I heard the familiar voice of one of the women who'd interviewed me during the audition process. 'George, I'm going to get straight to the point. We'd like to offer you a spot on *Australian Survivor* —'

'I ACCEPT YOUR OFFER!'

There are times in life where it's best to play it cool, but this wasn't one of them. She could have told me to do anything on that phone call and I would have said yes. My mind immediately went to the campy 2001 comedy film *Heartbreakers*, in which Sigourney Weaver plays a gold-digger who would marry older men to take their money. In one scene, a man close to death proposes to her, and her calculated reply is 'I accept your legally binding offer.'

That's how I felt on the phone – send me the papers right now, let me sign them, I don't care about lawyers, let's make this real! That casting call is the one that I had been waiting for since I was a teenager. I was making the jump from super fan and online *Survivor* player to actual, real-life tribemate. 'Overjoyed' didn't even begin to cut it.

There wasn't much else to say. She asked if I had any questions, but I could only think of one thing: whether or not I should have laser hair-removal before I competed, as I was quite hairy. (Alas, she did not have a firm opinion on the issue.) She told me they'd be back in touch with further details soon, and we said our goodbyes, me stupefied by my own smile.

I had finally made it. As I hung up the phone, I took a moment to bask in the pride of what I'd accomplished so far. *You did this, George. And you did it because you were the real you. George in all his glory.* The confidence wasn't faked any more. It was earned. I believed that I would make the cut, and I had.

Television, here I come.

CHAPTER 2

LOOK AFTER YOUR OWN

I like to reflect on what I am grateful for in life, and the opportunity to grow up in Bankstown makes me thankful more than anything else. I was born in Bankstown Hospital, attended Bankstown Public School and LaSalle Catholic College Bankstown, and completed my non-law university electives at the University of Western Sydney Bankstown Campus in Milperra. I still live in Bankstown to this day, in the same house I grew up in. I have spent no more than seven months of my life living outside of Bankstown, including all of my travel and television filming. You really can't get much more Bankstown than that.

The one thing you learn very quickly in Bankstown is to look after your people. You have to, otherwise no one else will. As I showed during my time on *Survivor* and throughout my professional career, if you are my friend and my ally, I will never let you go – and I expect all my kin to do the same for me.

I learned that from my parents, who have always looked after their own. As I write this, my mum is busy building a granny flat for my grandmother in the backyard of our family home, so that Yiayia can see out her final years on this earth just a few steps away from her daughter. A few years before that, my dad converted the house's garage into a fully functional hair salon so that my little sister, Pam, could start her dream business as a hairdresser with low overheads. And right now, I've taken over the top level of the house, with my 'temporary' COVID move to live back with the folks, giving me the ability to clear all my personal debt and save to buy a place of my own nearby. None of this is unusual in Bankstown, where family usually doesn't fly too far from the nest. We stick around to look after each other.

I love living in Bankstown, and I feel represented here. We're a town of immigrants – just 13 per cent of people in the Canterbury–Bankstown local government area ticked 'Australian' as their ancestry in the last census, compared to almost 30 per cent of Australians in general. Right now,

Lebanese, Chinese and Vietnamese top the percentages of ancestries represented in Bankstown, but that's always changing as new people settle here and put down roots. To look at it another way, a whopping 66 per cent of people in Bankstown have *both* parents born overseas – well above the national total of 36 per cent.

When you've grown up in Bankstown, you have a much broader perspective on what's important in life and what isn't. That's what happens when you're raised in a suburb largely consisting of people who've fled their home countries in search of a better life. For every resident, with my own family as an example, Bankstown has provided an opportunity to build a home and have an easier life.

Even its history is steeped in this multicultural mentality. Before European settlement, the land that we now call Bankstown was occupied by the Gadigal people of the Eora nation. The local Indigenous communities surrounded what we now know as the Cooks and Georges Rivers. (For the record, I support changing these names back to their original names rather than recognising colonial settlers who have no connection to the current people of Bankstown.) The area was known for its mostly turpentine-ironbark forest, unrecognisable from the densely populated concrete forest of houses, shops and roads it is today. In 1795, British colonisers Matthew Flinders and George Bass went exploring from the Georges River south of Sydney and came across the area, with Governor John Hunter establishing a pioneer colony there called Bank's Town, after botanist Sir Joseph Banks.

Some 150 years later, Bankstown found a new lease of life with a post-war population boom. After World War II, European immigrants and refugees fled from Macedonia, Serbia, Croatia, Italy, Greece, Poland and the Baltics, all mixing together to form a little mini-Europe 19 kilometres south-west of Sydney's CBD. Later, migrants and refugees arrived from even more countries, enriching the Bankstown community with their own cultures and customs: the Lebanese came after their civil war, the Vietnamese after the Vietnam War, then more recently people from West Africa.

My Aussie roots go back even earlier than that, though. Resettlement, disruption and perseverance define my family history. In the late 1920s, my great-grandfather – my father's father's father – migrated to Australia from Macedonia. His name was Done Koiovski and he made the move as a young man almost a decade after World War I ended.

The war had been difficult for the people of Macedonia, so Done left his home in search of more opportunity, landing first in Perth. In the 1920s, Perth would have been a big culture shock for a man from a rural village in Aegean Macedonia, within the borders of Greece. He would travel between Australia and Europe quite regularly, taking his earnings back to support his family. Some time in the 1930s, while on one of these trips, Done saw his wife, Dimitra, and sons for the first time in 10 years. Done returned to Perth in 1936 while his daughter Vicki was still in the womb. His wife and children would not migrate to Australia to be with him until the 1950s.

My grandfather Georgi was conceived during one visit, but stayed in Macedonia with his mother when he was born. He married my grandmother Parthena during the Greek Civil War, which ran from 1944 to 1949. By default, and without any political understanding, ethnic Macedonians like Georgi were placed on the side of the Communists. Parthena lived in the Macedonia region because her parents were ethnic Greek refugees who'd resettled after the Greek–Turkish population exchange of the 1920s.

After the Greek Civil War, Georgi and Parthena fled on foot through Albania, where they boarded a Soviet ship in Vlore they were told would take them to Russia. Instead, they would spend the next 11 years of their lives in Tashkent,

Uzbekistan, where Stalin sent other ethnic minorities to work. (Georgi died before I turned one, but I often wish I'd spoken to my grandmother about what life had been like in Soviet Uzbekistan.) My dad, Kris, was born in Tashkent and finally, in 1960, the family moved back to Yugoslav Macedonia when my father was just three.

Meanwhile, Done – now living in Bankstown – had spent the 1950s trying to track down his antipodean family members to bring them to Australia. The first person he found was my Aunt Vicki, who had spent her whole young life in an orphanage in Bucharest, Romania. He brought her to Australia when she was almost 18, and she now lives a quiet life in Sydney's picturesque northern beaches, far away from the difficulties of her childhood. Done's wife, Dimitra, soon followed.

In 1964, the Australian Red Cross alerted Done that his son, Georgi, was living as a stateless citizen in Yugoslav Macedonia. Done made contact, and eventually the entire family migrated to live with him in Bankstown. My family has never left. Done died about the same time my grandfather did in 1990, which meant that I never got the chance to know him. What I do know is that Georgi never let go of the fact that he grew up alone, through war and disruption, without his father.

I have very little recollection of my great-grandmother Dimitra. I recall being at her house on Brandon Avenue in Bankstown and being fascinated by the breakup of Yugoslavia, which was on the news in early 1992. (Three-year-old George already enjoyed complex geopolitics.) I also remember her big clock and a fluffy white companion dog – perhaps my inspiration to get my own fluffy white dog, Douglas, in 2016.

That's how my dad wound up in Bankstown: a multi-nation milieu that represents the story of many residents.

Mum's story isn't too different.

My mother, Maria, was born and raised in Marrickville, in Sydney's inner-west. Nowadays it's been thoroughly gentrified – a land of craft beers and vegan restaurants – but back when my mum was born in 1966, it was where all the working-class Greek migrants lived. Immigrants lived in terrace houses that now fetch multi-million-dollar sums, carving out new lives for themselves on the other side of the world from their home countries.

My mum's father, Stamatios, was born on the Greek island of Kalymnos. It's one of the easternmost Greek islands, situated about 10 kilometres from mainland Turkey. Stamatios had migrated to Australia in the mid-1950s, stopping first in Darwin for a couple of years, where he worked as a pearl diver, before settling in Sydney. My maternal grandmother, Panayota, moved to Sydney in the late 1950s from central Greece, and these two Greek immigrants met and fell in love. They might have both just been 'wogs' to the Anglo Aussies, but they were actually from areas of Greece almost 1000 kilometres and an Aegean Sea apart.

My parents were introduced by mutual friends one day in the early '80s, and despite Dad being 11 years Mum's senior, it was a classic love story typical of second-generations at the time. The match worked well in the eyes of my grandfather because, despite being ethnically Macedonian, my father and his entire family were fluent in Greek.

My dad wasn't the only one who grew up speaking multiple languages. By Year Three, I could string sentences together in Macedonian, Greek, Vietnamese and Arabic, some of them not particularly polite sentences. Most of my friends could, too. The kids in Bankstown ate bánh mì before it was cool, and would swap kebapi and ajvar for fried kebbe and toum.

WHEN YOU GROW UP IN BANKSTOWN, YOU INTUITIVELY HAVE AN ACCEPTANCE OF DIFFERENCE. IT'S INTRINSIC TO ASSESS PEOPLE ON THEIR CHARACTER, NOT THEIR ETHNICITY.

You like or dislike them based on whether they are a good person, not their race or colour. It was only when we visited each other's family homes that we realised how different some parts of our lives and upbringings were.

After-school trips to friends' houses would often be like stepping into another country for a few hours. Their parents and extended families often kept close ties to their homelands, so their domestic lives were filled with the smells, tastes and textures of faraway countries. It taught me the importance of being open-minded: of accepting and embracing cultural differences. It's a value I've carried into my career and certainly into my game on *Survivor* – drop me anywhere, with any group of people, and I believe I could find common ground and start to form friendships. It's an important quality to cultivate in life.

HOW ARE YOU GOING TO BUILD YOUR TRIBE IF YOU'RE DISCOUNTING PEOPLE BECAUSE THEY'RE DIFFERENT TO YOU?

Plus, when it comes to your friends and allies, casting your net wide will ensure you gain access to skills and life experiences you otherwise could never have. Take Thuan, one of my best mates since kindergarten, who was born in a Malaysian refugee camp after his parents fled South Vietnam on a boat.

I didn't befriend Thuan over the paste and pipe cleaners at kindie with any ulterior motives. But almost 30 years later, he's one of my most valuable allies. I cherish our lifelong friendship. My first overseas holiday was accompanying him to Vietnam, his guidance certainly easing the culture shock of navigating the roads there without getting mown down by a motorcycle.

But we've helped each other career-wise too. When my then-boss, Tania Mihailuk, was in need of a new casual staff member for her Bankstown office, I knew just who to call: Thuan, fresh out of uni and looking for work.

WHEN IT COMES TO YOUR
FRIENDS AND ALLIES,
CASTING YOUR NET WIDE
WILL ENSURE YOU GAIN
ACCESS TO SKILLS AND
LIFE EXPERIENCES YOU
OTHERWISE COULD
NEVER HAVE.

Bankstown has one of the highest proportions of Vietnamese people in Australia. Suddenly we had a professional young Vietnamese guy working the phones and meeting constituents in our office, speaking to them in their own language. A win for me as the office manager and for my boss, and a great career opportunity for Thuan. As you'll read again and again this book, there are many situations where you can benefit yourself and others. Did hiring Thuan help my career prospects? Yes. Did it help Thuan's? Also yes.

Of course, life's not always easy in Bankstown. My parents have always been low-income earners in the form of self-employed cleaners. I spent many an evening as a child sitting quietly in the corner of some empty doctor's room or office building, playing my Game Boy or reading a book while I waited patiently for Mum and Dad to finish cleaning.

That wasn't unusual among kids at my school, many of whom had parents who worked night jobs as cleaners or taxi drivers. I was just thankful I at least got to accompany my parents on their jobs to spend some time with them. Some of my friends would wave goodbye to a night-shift-working parent not long after they arrived home from school.

My parents are still cleaners to this day. Up until very recently, they cleaned one of the local Vietnamese restaurants every single night after it shut. Coming in at 9pm, scrubbing tirelessly until the job was done – usually around midnight – every night for 20 years. That's a hard life, but they've never complained. My parents are typical of many in Bankstown: working hard and doing whatever it takes to provide for their families.

It therefore frustrates me that 'Bankstown' is a bit of a dirty word in some areas of Sydney. I'm sure you have suburbs like that wherever you live: the place in the city that's full of working-class people and immigrants. We have a few here across Western Sydney. I think it's another reason why people from Western Sydney tend to support each other when needed. We know we're the underdogs, so we have each other's backs.

What disappoints me is that Bankstown still doesn't get its fair share of resources. At a both a State and Federal level, Bankstown and its surrounding suburbs are safe Labor seats, and it's to our detriment – it means there isn't the political impetus to get us the sort of funding needed to improve the quality of life of local residents.

Paul Keating is from Bankstown. The former prime minister is known for his frank views – particularly since retirement – and his strength to make the correct decisions no matter how difficult the circumstances. Keating and I went to the same high school, LaSalle Catholic College on Chapel Road in Bankstown. A signed biography of Keating sat in the school library, and every day I walked past it I would tell myself, 'If Keating can make a go of it, then so can I.'

I was lucky to work for an extremely hard-working former Member for Bankstown, Tania Mihailuk, who also grew up in the area. But not all Bankstown MPs are like Tania and Paul. Some are careerist politicians who have never lived a minute in the community and have neither the understanding nor desire to improve Bankstown.

The fact that Bankstown is taken for granted by politicians frustrates me immensely. In fact, it's a big part of why I joined the Labor party in the first place: I could see that things needed changing in my hometown, and I wanted to help.

I think my attitude is indicative of a change I've really noticed in this newer generation in Bankstown. Our parents and grandparents were focused on the hard scrabble of life: settling into a new country, making a go of things for themselves and building a family. They lived by the mantra of 'Be thankful for what you've got and don't, under any circumstances, complain.' After all, you could have it so much worse.

I am grateful to have had a loving and supporting family growing up, with parents who didn't earn a lot of money but made sure that their children could have happy lives. Thanks to the hard work of immigrant families like theirs, young people in Bankstown are immensely proud of their hometown – but they can also sometimes see that they're getting a raw deal.

You've got to demand what you're entitled to in life. If we, the people of Bankstown, don't do it, then nobody will do it for us. I look around and see younger people in Bankstown asking important questions about what's fair and equitable, and why their local community isn't getting a bigger piece of the pie.

But we fight for what we deserve. You non-Bankstownians could learn a thing or two from us: a few lessons on the importance of family, loyalty and pride. Being from Bankstown teaches you many things: it gives you grounding and perspective, it provides you with street smarts and good intuition and most importantly for me, it made me realise very early in my life that the people you surround yourself with are invaluable.

Growing up in Bankstown taught me something you will never learn in school:

KEEP YOUR FAMILY CLOSE, STAY LOYAL TO THE FRIENDS YOU FIND AND BE PROUD OF WHERE YOU'VE COME FROM.

If you can manage this as a start, then you will have a good foundation from which to make friends and manipulate people.

BUILD A TEAM OF LOYAL ALLIES

Loyalty is crucial for any strong friendship. I've gone through a few reinventions so far in my life, manoeuvring through the worlds of politics, poker and reality television, and the loyalty and support of a few trusted allies has been key in getting me where I am today.

Without loyalty, friendship means nothing. It's the foundation that builds a sense of trust and reliability between two people, safe in the knowledge that you're both there for the good *and* bad times.

And you can find it in some surprising places. I never could've expected that my most loyal ally on my first season

WITHOUT LOYALTY, FRIENDSHIP MEANS NOTHING.

of *Survivor* – and the closest friend I've made in the show – would be a blonde, well-to-do woman from one of Sydney's most exclusive harbourside suburbs.

On paper, Cara Atchison and I had very little in common, but within minutes of laying eyes on each other in the Australian Outback, we realised we were kindred spirits and needed to work together.

She works as a real-estate agent selling luxury properties in Double Bay. The eastern suburb has earned the nickname 'Double Pay' among Sydneysiders as the properties are so expensive there, even compared to other Sydney prices; Fairwater, a grand one-hectare estate, smashed all records when it sold for $100 million back in 2018. (Unfortunately, Cara didn't sell that one – she would've loved the commission.) Her clientele are the well-heeled social set of Sydney's eastern suburbs, who cluster around a select few tiny suburbs – Point Piper, Darling Point, Vaucluse – filling their large houses with priceless artworks, their driveways with luxury cars and their foreheads with Botox.

There can be a real divide between Sydney's east and west; residents of both areas rarely have reason to be on each other's home turfs. Had it not been for *Survivor*, I'm not sure I ever would've crossed paths with Cara. The luxury harbourside properties she sells are not exactly in my price range, so I definitely wouldn't have met her through her work.

I remember exactly what I thought when she introduced herself to me in the dust and dirt of Outback Cloncurry: She looks like a wealthy, retired tennis player. But within five minutes of meeting her, I realised there was a lot more to Cara, and that she was going to be an important person for my game.

For a start, this Double Bay duchess was actually born and raised in Campbelltown – a suburb in Sydney's south-west not hugely dissimilar to Bankstown. Like me, she'd always been highly motivated to succeed. For me, that had led to success in the political sphere, and for her, that led to building one of the most prestigious real-estate businesses in Australia.

Beyond our shared Westie roots, we quickly realised that we had the same outlook on life, too. Cara and I may have had very different bank accounts and lifestyles, but having a similar drive and determination is what bonded us when we didn't have much else.

It's important to look beneath the surface when determining if you want to align yourself with someone. If I'd made a snap judgement about Cara on that first day at camp, I might have kept my distance. Instead, we gazed beyond that and considered what we were both like as people.

PAYCHEQUES AND POSTCODES ARE ALL VERY WELL, BUT WHAT DOES THIS PERSON REALLY BELIEVE? WHAT ARE THEIR VALUES? THAT'S WHERE YOU'RE LOOKING FOR AN ALIGNMENT.

With Cara, I very quickly realised that we were the same where it mattered: loyalty.

The way Cara spoke glowingly about her family and her children back home made me realise what a devoted wife and mother she is to them. Her pride and love for them was evident in her eyes. *Survivor* can be a lonely old game, so I think absent our friends and family we were both only too happy to enter into an intense new friendship together in the Outback.

We had each other's backs throughout the game, sharing information and working closely together. At one point, I even saved her life. It was the middle of the night at camp, and we were all asleep. It got super-cold out there in the desert at night, so we all slept close to the fire; Cara and I usually huddled together for extra body warmth. It must've been 2 or 3am when I randomly woke up for a second – at the exact moment embers from the fire landed on Cara's duffle bag, right near her head. Suddenly, a flame ignited.

'Cara! Wake up, wake up! Your hair's on fire!' I screamed, jolting the whole camp awake.

I leapt to my feet and smothered the flame. She was singed and spooked, but otherwise unharmed. I shudder to think how bad it could've been had I not opened my eyes at that exact moment. I like to think the *Survivor* gods were looking down, giving me a nudge to make sure I protected my number-one ally.

After I saved her life – and no, I've never let her forget it – she also saved mine. In a manner of speaking. Her selfless act was the first time King George cried in the game of *Survivor*.

It was tribal council on our 14th day in the game. Cara had struck *Survivor* gold a few days earlier: together we'd found a much-needed immunity idol in a tree after hunting for several days on the down-low. In life, just like in *Survivor*, sometimes people are gifted an opportunity to assert control or to favour themselves. In the game, this is what a hidden immunity idol can do. This necklace can save you from being voted off at the tribal council where you play it, either for yourself or, in some circumstances, another player.

At the time we were in an alliance with a guy called Baden

and a woman called Wai – but she had just told us that she was leaving our minority alliance and voting for me. It was devastating – a betrayal by a former ally who I had saved in the game on Day Two. From there, Cara, Baden and I hatched a last ditch plan: we'd pass the idol between us like a hot potato at tribal council, leaving those who wanted to vote us out with no clue as to who they should target. But we understood that if Cara decided to play her idol, it would be for herself. It was her idol, after all.

It was a heated and emotional tribal council. Cara spoke about what mattered to people in business and life: loyalty, integrity and standing for something. I gave an impassioned valedictory speech knowing the end was near. Baden, who is a former Tour de France winner, spoke about sticking up for your mates and allies.

As planned, we threw the idol around publicly to keep the majority guessing. Cara gave the idol to Baden halfway through the tribal. I was voting first, so Baden then gave the idol to me. I considered having a villainous *Survivor* moment while wearing Cara's idol. It was in my possession at the final minute, and I could play it for myself. But I would never do that to Cara. I gave it back to her and put on my backpack, ready to leave the game instead.

When time came to count the votes, Jonathan LaPaglia uttered the immortal words: 'If anybody has a hidden immunity idol they would like to play, now would be the time to do so.'

Cara stood up, approached JLP, and announced she'd be playing her idol … for me.

The second she said it, tears started to well in my eyes.

'Why did you do that?' I gasped as she sat back down next to me.

'Because I wanted to,' she said, with a shrug and a smile. She offered three more words by way of explanation: 'I'm a mum.'

The votes were called: four for me, none of which counted, three for Cara and three for another player, Georgia. Cara had been right – if she hadn't played that idol for me, I would have been a goner.

But because she had protected me, she had now put herself in danger. Because it was a tie, that meant an agonising wait for a revote. We all once more took turns going up to the voting booth, except this time, we were only allowed to vote for either Cara or Georgia.

Throughout it all, Cara stayed her calm, serene self, even as the new votes were read. I knew in my gut what was going to happen, and I was right: The majority alliance openly called Baden, Cara and me the 'misfits,' put all their votes on Cara, and I shed more tears as JLP called her name as the next contestant voted out.

In saving me, Cara had sacrificed herself. How's that for loyalty? Our friendship had been so intense that when her torch was snuffed, it really felt like she was giving up her life for me.

'You're so selfless,' I whimpered through tears as she said her goodbyes. I held her for what I thought would be the last time in the game.

I stood by that Brains campfire for hours that night making tributes to Cara as if it were a funeral, while some of my tribemates sneered at me with laughter. The camp suddenly felt much colder sleeping next to Baden, who wasn't a fan of sharing body warmth on the single-digit temperature evenings. It didn't help that he had a $2000 leather jacket for his wardrobe, while I had a $20 Hawaiian dog shirt.

Thankfully, in a twist none of us knew about, it was a non-elimination episode, and when Cara left tribal council, she was instead given a 'Brawn' Buff and told she'd be switching sides. I didn't know that at the time, so while I was sulking in the dirt, Cara was living it up at the much more pleasant Brawn camp.

I only realised that Cara was back in the game at the next challenge. Jonathan muttered the words, 'Brains, have a look at the new Brawn tribe,' but to me it still hadn't clicked because Cara was disguised in another tribe member's clothes.

But when she waved to me, it gave me hope. I could see a slim path forward in the game if Cara and I could eventually be reunited. I knew more than anything else I had a rock more immovable than Gibraltar in my best friend Cara.

Eventually, Cara would make it to the season's top four alongside me. We ended up voting for each other in a moment we knew was happening, but couldn't bear to acknowledge. It meant I would make the Final Two with Hayley Leake, the Australian Queen and a lifelong friend, but in hindsight I wish I hadn't done it.

I still get teary to this day if I watch Cara's selfless tribal council gesture back. It is the nicest thing anyone's ever done for me. That night, she thought she was sacrificing herself to save me. Why did she do it? We've both been asked that question a lot in the years since.

While Cara saved me mostly out of love, there was also strategy involved. We were both at the bottom of our tribe at the time, and those targeting us had made it known that they'd pick us off in order of who was weakest in challenges.

They considered Cara the weakest, so her thinking was: why save myself tonight, only to be sent home tomorrow? Better to give the lifeline to George, who can get back to camp and try to hustle himself a bit further in the game.

But if we hadn't laid the groundwork of loyalty and lasting friendship already, she never would have done it. After all, only 14 days earlier we had been complete strangers. *Survivor* is a high-pressure situation, and from that pressure, our diamond of a friendship was quickly formed.

YOU SEE PEOPLE'S TRUEST COLOURS WHEN THEIR BACK IS AGAINST THE WALL.

Years earlier, one of the best times in my life came with a formation of a different kind: the creation of the Western Sydney Wanderers Football Club in 2012. I was in my early twenties and football-mad, and as the newly formed club got a groundswell of community support, I felt like I suddenly found my tribe: friends with the same common interest, bonding over their love of the game and being from Western Sydney.

My friend Sean is an unusual character. He's a sparky who loves the outdoors and being on the move; wanderlust never keeps him in one place for too long. I found out where he got these traits from once we drove up to far north Queensland to watch a Wanderers away game and stayed with his mum, who lives off the grid – no electricity, no running water and a long-drop toilet.

Despite some clear lifestyle differences, Sean and I shared similar values (on top of our love of football): independence, being principled and staying positive.

A few years into our friendship, Sean was on the move once more, escaping Sydney due to the high cost of living and moving in with his mum. I was always tickled by the irony of a qualified electrician choosing to live in a house without connection to the electricity grid – Sean, help your mum out! We kept in regular contact, and when he drove back down to surprise me for my birthday, he confessed that he was missing the Sydney rat race and was keen to come back.

I knew he'd previously left the city because of the soaring cost of living. I knew it would be hard to break back into Sydney's housing and job markets. But I also knew my friend was in need – and that's how Sean came to live in the spare bedroom of my unit, rent-free, for several months while he sorted himself out a job and found a place of his own to call home. Sean was – and still is – one of my closest friends, and

I know he'll repay the favour tenfold when he can. (He keeps on telling me to come up and sleep on his mum's couch for a couple of months in return, but as I've told him, the only way I'll live in the tropics with no proper air-con or toilets is if I've got a shot at winning half a million dollars at the end of it.)

But his loyalty remains. As I travelled to Cloncurry for the first season of *Survivor*, I spent several nights in a hotel room in Townsville. I knew I'd be in pre-season lockdown and unable to leave my hotel room or tell anyone what I was doing so far from Bankstown. But I also knew I was going to be closer to Sean than I had been in a long time, so I thought it would be fun to let him know.

'Sean,' I texted. 'I'm going to be spending a night in Townsville. I'll be in hotel lockdown though, so don't bother coming to visit. Long story.'

He wouldn't take no for an answer. He drove three hours from his home into Townsville and stood on the street under my hotel room, waving and screaming. This is typical crazy Sean. With my *Survivor* minders lurking, we couldn't catch up, share stories or even a simple hug. I couldn't even yell back – I was several storeys up, and shouting down to him would see a very quick knock at my door with a stern reminder about pre-*Survivor* isolation rules, maybe even a boot from the game before it had started.

So instead, we just waved and manically grinned at each other. His was the last familiar face I saw before I entered the competition and it helped me focus for the game ahead. For that I'm grateful – *that's* a loyal ally.

My friendships with both Sean and Cara continue to this day. In fact, we were responsible for a *Survivor* first.

Before each season starts, players have to nominate a member or two from their family who will fly out to support them if they make it to the final immunity challenge. I'd had my mum and sister fill that slot on my first season, and while I love them dearly, they didn't exactly give me the kind of tough love I needed in that moment. After my first of five hours in a torture rack, every bone of my body aching, my mum yelled: 'It's OK, George! You can come down now.' That's the kind of loving support you want at the dinner table after a bad day in the office, but not what you want to hear in a final immunity endurance challenge with $500,000 on the line.

It's not their fault; it's just that I've always been open with my parents about wanting to pay off the remainder of their mortgage if I ever won *Survivor*. When I didn't win the final immunity challenge in that first season, I found it hard to look at my mum, disappointed my failure had made that dream feel further out of reach. That's not the 'I'm a winner' feeling you want going into a final tribal council.

To me, Cara was the better option: a bright, sunny cheerleader who'd keep me motivated with catcalls like 'Go Georgey! You're going to shout us lunch at Catalina when you win this!' She kept my spirits high and kept my eyes on the prize (which she seemed to think was oysters at a *very expensive* restaurant). She was exactly the friend I needed in that moment, and so she became the first player to return as 'family' for another contestant.

That final immunity challenge in Samoa – named 'Uncomfortably Numb' – was just the sort of medieval implement of torture I dread on *Survivor*. We final four contestants had to balance on narrow poles, spikes operated by a ye-olde hand crank pushing further into our backs at regular intervals. The pain was immense.

I tried my best in these sorts of challenges, but I always silently wanted someone else to hurry up and win so I could go back to having full facility of my limbs. That day, I came a respectable third place, lasting three hours up there before I gingerly limped off the pole about 15 minutes before the winner. I was nursing a shoulder injury the entire game, and just my luck it was a shoulder-based endurance challenge. I was crushed, but there was Cara, still cheering and telling me what an amazing job I'd done.

Even though I didn't win, once we were back in Sydney, I took her for that lunch at Catalina.

She'd be my one phone call if I ever went to prison, the friend I know would put her hand up to donate a kidney. Our friendship is for life, and that's because it was forged in a high-stress environment where we proved our loyalty to each other quickly through our words and our actions.

I'll give you a bunch of shortcuts and cheap tricks throughout this book that will help you get your way – but there's only way you can build a faithful team of supporters who are willing to go in to bat for you: You have to first put in the groundwork, and make sure you look after them. That's what a good friendship is built on.

SELFLESS ACTS BREED LOYALTY.

Choose wisely, though. Pick your targets when it comes to offering generosity and loyalty. You're unlikely to win any lasting friendships by walking into a pub and announcing you're buying everyone a round of drinks. Sure, you'll probably earn a round of applause, and maybe a few drunken chats, but the interaction is transactional. It's not based on any shared goals or interests (other than beer).

Find your Caras, your Seans, then show them that you'll look after them. If you do, you're on your way to gathering a tribe of loyal allies.

WIN FRIENDS – AND EMPTY THEIR WALLETS

Relatively early on in my life, I developed a passion for a game that would marry the two goals that that form the very title of this book: winning friends and manipulating people. Play your cards right (pun intended), and you can make new mates who'll literally pay you for the privilege.

That game is poker. At its very essence, poker is a game of maths and numbers. If you can master the strategy behind the probability of certain known cards that may come out of the deck, you have a distinct chance of winning a hand. Of course, the beauty of poker is that it gives players the opportunity to bluff their way to success, by buying the pot in front of them when they do not have the winning hand.

There are many poker strategy books out there – and this is not one of them – but what I'm more interested in is applying the lessons I've learned from poker to life off the table.

My poker journey started in a random but appropriate place: the back row of Mr Farag's Year 9 Advanced Maths class at LaSalle Catholic College in Bankstown.

Mr Farag was a blunt Egyptian man who was prone to volcanic eruptions whenever he felt you weren't paying sufficient attention to his favourite subject: advanced high-school mathematics. It was enough to make you wet yourself, and many of us almost did. You'd be lulled into a near-coma, eyes going droopy, as he turned his back to the class, droning on about trigonometry and graph linear equations and writing endless strings of numbers on the board. Then, a giggle or a private conversation near you would prick his ear, and he'd spin around, ready to destroy.

'GET OUT OF MY CLASSROOM!' he'd yell at the offender.

It was a discombobulating experience – coma, coma, coma, *SCREAMING!!!*, coma, coma.

Fortunately, we students did have the edge on Mr Farag, who was both hard of hearing and short of vision. He usually removed his thick spectacles when he was in class, and we soon worked out that anyone in the back row had a little more leeway – we seemed to be both out of his earshot and vision. Sit in the front row, and he'd scream at you for sneezing. Sit in the back row, and you had the freedom to ... oh, I don't know, set up an underground poker ring?

I was good at maths, but I knew that I had no intention of keeping it up as I went for my Higher School Certificate exams. I was more interested in applying my maths acumen to more *practical* pursuits.

One day, I brought a deck of cards to school. My interest in the game had been sparked by chance one night. I was a teenager who loved staying up late and watching TV when I should've been asleep in bed before the next day of school. In the early hours of one morning, after watching ab-roller infomercials and whatever foreign-language movie happened to be on SBS, I channel-surfed my way onto a televised poker tournament.

I was immediately intrigued – as were a lot of other people around the world at that time. This was the era poker suddenly had its glow-up, going from being played by fictional gangsters in the back rooms of smoky bars to attracting the minds of millions of everyday people looking to test their luck and skill to live a tangible poker dream.

It all started in 2003 with an unassuming American accountant by the name of Chris Moneymaker (yes, that is his real name!). He managed to qualify for the Main Event of the World Series of Poker, which is the biggest poker tournament in the world. But he didn't do this by playing the casino circuit for months in the lead-up, earning his place against the game's best – he paid $86 and won an online poker tournament to seal his spot. He was an unknown wildcard, and it was his first-ever live poker tournament; he had mostly played on his computer at home before heading to Vegas.

That year, Moneymaker beat the other 838 players in the field to take home first prize: $2.5 million dollars. His massive win shone a spotlight on poker and told the fairy-tale story that any regular guy living in the suburbs could become a multimillionaire overnight, just by knowing his way around 52 cards. The following year, 2576 people entered the World Series Main Event, and the year after that, when Aussie Joe Hachem claimed victory, there were more than 5600 in the competition. Sports historians now call this 'the Moneymaker effect,' and it revolutionised the game.

But the impact Moneymaker's win had on poker itself was far bigger than just the main event. It became a popular game both online and in living rooms across the world, with plenty of people – including me – dreaming of being the next moneymaking Moneymaker.

Which brings me back to Mr Farag's maths class. Too young to play in pubs or clubs, I had to make do with school. And what better place to stage the inaugural LaSalle Catholic College tournament than the classroom that first taught me about odds and statistics?

We played in the back row. It was a cash game, playing with gold coins I had exchanged from a $20 dollar note I broke down at the school canteen. It was thrilling every time someone won a dollar, but we had to be discreet, as not to awaken Mr Farag's infamous temper.

Cards were stealthily dealt whenever Farag's attention was on the blackboard. We'd stay as silent as we could – win a hand, and all you could do was smile, logging the victory in your brain so you could properly gloat once you were outside in the schoolyard.

From there, the game grew, and the back-row game with four LaSalle boys moved to the playground. Other students wanted in, which also helped me get to know the rest of my classmates – including which ones I could win the most money from. You're a choir kid who has never taken an accounting class? Come on in! A politics buff who doesn't know how fractions work? Take a seat. When playing at school, we had to be careful not to be too blatant, keeping watch for teachers. My poker ring probably wouldn't register for the more clueless among them – 'Oh, how nice, those boys are playing UNO!' – but I knew if a more clued-in one saw us during school times, we'd be toast. It got to the point where I knew I had to take it off school grounds before someone got wise to the operation and put me out of business. So I moved the games to a more comfortable setting to support the wider pool of players: my parents' house.

By the time I was in Year 12, I had roped in around 70 of the 110 boys in my year to be a part of my poker stable. It was a whole operation, with me at the helm. Instead of doing practice exams, I ran regular afterschool and weekend cash games out of the spare dining room on the second storey of my family's house in Bankstown. The room looked then as it does now—and in fact as it did 30 years earlier, when it was built and furnished in 1980. It's like a design time capsule, decorated in browns and beiges. The players sat around our large circular dining table, all relieved that we could actually relax and enjoy a game without the constant threat of being sprung by Mr Farag or a teacher on playground duty.

The cash game was a real boon for me on a personal level.

I WAS WINNING MONEY, SURE, BUT ALSO WINNING FRIENDS.

Most of the guys coming to play had never played poker before or were enjoying the buzz after Joe Hachem won the World Series of Poker, being the first Aussie to do so.

Students I'd barely spoken to throughout the entirety of high school were suddenly eager to score an invite to George's house for a poker game. Cards brought everyone together: the science nerds, the football jocks, the social crowd. What had started as a way to pass the time in the back row of maths class had grown into a little suburban utopia. Teenagers were always fiercely tribal in the school yard, but they put their differences aside in my family's dining room so they could enjoy the game.

And at the middle of it all: me, running the whole operation. Of course, I wasn't just doing all this to create some blissed-out Hollywood scene of high-school unity. I was also making bank.

By this stage, I had had read several poker-strategy books, and I was a far more advanced player than anybody coming to my home game. I had my Year 12 homework to get through each night, but on top of that, I gave myself poker homework, staying up late to watch those televised tournaments and reading whatever I could about the game online.

Poker, at its essence, is a game of two factors: probability and certainty. The probability component comes down to the nature of a deck of cards, which are shuffled and come out in a random order. The certainty of it is around the fact that you, as a poker player, know what you are dealing with: 52 cards in a deck, two cards in each player's hand and three cards coming at the flop (that's the term for the dealing of the first three face-up cards to the board). From there, an additional card is dealt a second and a third time, with players betting on their likelihood of winning at the end of each reveal. At the end of all betting rounds, the player who has the best hand (and has not folded) wins all the money that's been bet, which is known as the 'pot'.

UNDERSTANDING PROBABILITY AND CERTAINTY WHILE PLAYING POKER HONES SO MANY SKILLS YOU CAN TRANSFER TO OTHER SITUATIONS.

Skilled poker players become masters at weighing up risk versus reward elsewhere in life: figuring out whether you should quit that job, buy that house, start that business. A good poker player will have the skills to run the pros and cons calmly and rationally in high-stress situations, while many people get blinded by either the negative ('I could never afford the mortgage') or the positive ('It has a claw-foot bathtub!').

This extra bit of understanding about the two elements at play in poker gave me the edge against my Year 12 schoolmates, who were coming in droves to the Mladenov household mini-tournaments to try their hand at the game. I was taking it all a little more seriously than most of my opponents (not that I let that on).

The buy-in to play was usually set at $50, and there were usually eight players in a game. That meant a prize of $250 for the tournament winner and a token $100 for second and $50 for third – all pretty serious money for a high schooler almost 20 years ago. My fellow players would save up for weeks, pooling the lunch money they got from their parents with the pittance they earned from part-time jobs in takeaway stores or retail in Bankstown Square, just for a chance to play. I'm sure there were a few upset parents when their kids returned from a game at my house penniless and in need of a new cash injection for tomorrow's lunch. Meanwhile, I could have bought the whole grade a processed spicy tandoori chicken burger with what I was pulling in.

My greater understanding of the mathematics behind poker coupled with my awareness of when to bet and when to fold ensured I was almost always going to land on top.

BUT NO ONE WANTS TO PLAY A GAME IF THEY NEVER WIN, DO THEY?

That's why I deliberately set this three-tiered winner structure, because the three cash prizes on offer gave enough incentive for the other players to keep coming back for more. I almost always ended up with cash in my pocket – but I wasn't the only one making dough. Not that the prize pool even mattered to everyone, as a lot of people just came for the laughs. Some would win money, some would not, but they were guaranteed a good time.

I was in my element. Making new mates, emptying their wallets and earning enough in this side hustle to not need to work a part-time job while at school. I was itching to take my love of poker further: from the back row of maths class, to the upstairs living room at my family home, to actual pubs and clubs.

The day I turned 18, I walked into Bankstown Sports Club – not to eat at LaPiazza Italian Bistro with my family, as I'd done a thousand times, but rather to saunter deeper into the bowels of the massive complex to try my luck at poker.

It felt like I'd finally graduated. Now I was at the big boys' table, down past the rows and rows of pokie machines, in a poker room I'd never seen the inside of, despite all the other times I'd come here. It was hidden in the old downstairs bar, which is now a brewery.

The venue would hold tournaments twice weekly, on Wednesdays and Sundays. When I registered to play an Australian Poker League event for the first time, entry was free. The grand prize? $150, less than my home tournament. Still, I was every bit as nervous as I'm sure Moneymaker had been when he was playing for millions on the final table in Vegas.

I wasn't warmly welcomed at that first game. Here I was, a newly legal, fresh-faced 18-year-old, overly eager to play with people who'd been sat at that table for longer than I'd been alive. I was like the golden retriever in a dog park full of judgemental bulldogs. Initially, it was jarring: the easy laughs and camaraderie of my after-school tournaments seemed to be missing. (Then again, I was often playing with Greek pensioners, rather than teenagers.) But I persisted, keen to properly make my mark as an adult poker player.

I was surprised by what I saw when I started competing at the semi-pro level in the Australian Poker League. Poker requires you to gain a mental edge over your opponent, but to my mind, you don't want to be seen as doing so. Some players in these tournaments loved showing their cards after they'd successfully bluffed another competitor, rubbing their faces in the deception. But if you've successfully fooled somebody, why break the hard-earned ruse?

To this day, I've never understood it.

When a game is all about what you know and what your opponents don't, what's the point in surrendering information voluntarily? Better to leave them in the dark so they never actually know whether you beat them fairly or you just pulled off a great poker swindle. Similarly, I've learned never to reveal my bluff. If I won on a fluke, that should be my little secret – nobody else needs to know that it was a lucky break.

WHEN YOU SCORE A WIN, ALWAYS LET PEOPLE BELIEVE IT WAS YOUR SMARTS THAT GOT YOU THERE.

After all, riding your luck to victory – that takes true smarts.

There were all types of people at these tournaments. The old blokes who hung around the pub all day, people coming back from the CBD still in their business attire, and tradies you could see shuffling their chips with their paint-stained fingers. The other thing my high-school training ground had taught me was to take the social game as seriously as the card game. Simply being nice and friendly to people is an undervalued skill. It costs nothing to be nice to people, and in a game where you're trying to get other people to do what you want, having them like you is certainly more beneficial than the alternative. A veneer of friendliness goes a long way (and can be a great cover for sneakiness).

I wasn't the only one using this tack. Some would go out of their way to be friendly, and during the scheduled breaks in tournaments I got to know plenty of them. Some of them came to be, and still are, friends off the poker table.

SIMPLY BEING NICE AND
FRIENDLY TO PEOPLE IS
AN UNDERVALUED SKILL.
A VENEER OF FRIENDLINESS
GOES A LONG WAY (AND
CAN BE A GREAT COVER
FOR SNEAKINESS).

But there were some people, for whatever reason, who saw no benefit to being friendly. These were the kinds of nasty characters who, without a second thought, would berate anyone for misplaying a hand. Again, this made no sense to me – if you thought someone was terrible at poker, why would you want to bully them away? Why abuse them and risk them never coming back? You *want* the bad players there.

IN FACT, THE MORE BAD PLAYERS AT THE TABLE, THE HIGHER CHANCES OF *YOU* WINNING. YOU WANT THE FISH AT THE TABLE WHEN YOU ARE A SHARK.

Of course you want to be the best player at the table, or at the very least one of the best. But you don't want to telegraph how good you are to anyone else. I can't stand people who act as though they are above others at the table, not only because they are unpleasant to be around, but because they have undoubtedly chased away less-talented players for good. I want the diversity – I want to increase my chances of winning against a newbie. I got in plenty of arguments with these prickly punters over the years, but rarely lost my cool to the extent where I wanted to flip the table.

I soon became a much-loved regular in the Western Sydney poker scene, and this worked in my favour. The locals in Bankstown and Revesby liked me because I was one of them. Everyone else liked me because I knew what I was doing, and was pleasant to be around – and when people want you at their poker table, guess what? They start letting you win hands, or folding to your bluffs when they might call against someone else.

Poker taught me – and still teaches me – so many valuable skills that I've been able to use away from the poker table. But above all, the most valuable lesson poker gave me is that you can widen your social circle while also using the situation to your own advantage. It's what the game's all about: fun, forging new friendships, and going home with those new friends' money in your pockets.

CHAPTER 5

USE CRITICISM AS AN OPPORTUNITY

I gave myself something of an emergency boot camp before my first season of *Survivor*. I'd been stressed, bored at my government policy job, overworked and eating unhealthy food, and as a result I was tipping the scales at around 95 kilograms. I was happy and living my best life – but not in the physical condition required to do well on a gruelling show like *Survivor*.

Once it looked like I might actually have a shot at competing on a show that sees contestants spend three nights a week plugged into living rooms across the nation usually wearing little more than their bathers, I knew I had to make some lifestyle changes. It wasn't just vanity – although that was definitely part of it – but a genuine concern about how I'd go with the game's tough athletic challenges if I didn't whip myself into shape a bit.

Beyond how my body looked on television, I also had to make sure I was fit enough to even make it on. *Survivor* players have to complete a few physical tests before they're cleared for the show. Most of it is pretty unchallenging stuff, checking that you're at least mobile enough to have a go at the show's challenges. There's a weight test, showing you can lift a 10 kilogram weight from the ground to your shoulder; a push-up test, where you're given one minute to do 10 push-ups (with your knees on the ground, to make it even easier); and a run test, which gives you 20 minutes to hit 1600 metres on a treadmill (which you can do in that time without even breaking into a light jog).

It's just enough to let the producers know that you're not going to cark it out there on their watch. I assume they don't really test your physical limits too much so they can have a diverse pool of people to pull from when casting the show. (I'm sure a *Survivor: Personal Trainers v Fitness Influencers* season would be nice to look at, but can you imagine the campfire convos? Snore.)

I passed most of the physical tests easily, but I was stressed about one I haven't mentioned yet: the swim test, in which you have to swim 200 metres non-stop. I'd never been a confident swimmer, and I was worried that without a bit of training I'd need to get rescued at about the halfway mark. Humiliating.

I practised twice before my swim test: once at Auburn pool, where I paddled with the Swim Sisters (formerly Burkini Babes) and couldn't make the distance. I blamed the unfamiliar location for my lack of swimming endurance. I then went to my local pool at Birrong, where I accidently ingested some of the pool water on my doggy paddle to the 50-metre mark, where the combination of chlorine water, the quinoa I'd eaten an hour prior and acid reflex found its way out of my mouth and into Birrong pool. My only saving grace was that there wasn't a film crew there to record it, only a bunch of bored teenagers on their phones.

But then it was time for the big league. I remember before my actual swim test that I clarified a number of times that the stroke did not matter and that there was not a time limit. This was important, because I knew my only hope of hitting the 200-metre mark was to paddle the whole way. And after about nine excruciating minutes splashing about like my Maltese terrier Douglas, I finished my fourth lap of 50 metres and knew that there would not be any barrier to my participation on Brains v Brawn in 2020.

The COVID-19 pandemic clearly had other ideas.

The period of the first COVID-19 lockdown in 2020 was particularly tough for me, not only due to the uncertainty of the pandemic at the time, but because I thought my golden ticket to *Australian Survivor* had been devastatingly taken away from me. When the first Sydney lockdown ended in June 2020, I convinced myself that the production of *Survivor* could pick up at any minute and I had to get my body ready, 'just in case'.

Having jumped the first COVID hurdle (though thank God I didn't have to literally go over any), it was time to start preparing my physique in earnest. Though I was happy with how I looked at the time, I wasn't all 'relaxed muscle', as much as I tried to tell myself that. I joined a local gym, made a great bunch of new friends, and started becoming a dedicated gym member for the first time in my life. My day was constructed around going to the morning or night class, six times a week.

In October 2020, a small glimmer of hope came in the form of an email from a member of the *Survivor* crew, asking whether I was still interested in taking part. My only hesitation in responding was whether I did it immediately or waited a few hours before replying with my definite yes.

By the time January 2021 rolled by, the casting ball was in full swing again, and picked up right where it left off a year prior. In this 12-month period, I had shed 20 kilograms of body fat and put on five kilograms of muscle according to the body scans I would take in between seven-week challenges.

I might not have been an athlete, but after becoming an F45 cult member, I had sweated and moved my body into the best shape I had ever been in my life. I felt strong and fit and that is all that mattered to me. I felt ready for *Survivor*: strong and healthy.

Turns out, it wasn't enough for the members of the Brawn tribe and the audience watching at home.

I did my best in Cloncurry, where the conditions were the most brutal of any *Survivor* location ever filmed, with wildly fluctuating temperatures, close to zero at night and 50°C during the day. When I saw a physical challenge that I knew I wasn't going to win, I decided to conserve what little energy I had and put it into running the numbers and being active in camp.

This was the right tactical decision for my gameplay, illustrated by making it to the final podium. But in life and

Survivor, perception is everything, and the public consensus was that I either didn't try hard enough or was a quitter. I think my biggest public humiliation came in one water-based challenge, when one by one, we had to leap off a high platform, reaching out to try and grab a key hanging from a rope a good few metres away before plummeting about ten metres into the dam below.

It looked so easy to the viewers at home (and boy, did they love to tell us on that social media after the episode finished airing). But having seen similar challenges on *Survivor* before, where contestants flail in the air nowhere close to the key before dropping like a sack of spuds and faceplanting painfully into the water below, I froze. I knew I wasn't going to win individual immunity, and the risk of injury at the final stage of the game after I had asserted political control through an alliance wasn't worth it – or so I reasoned to myself.

I don't like heights. And I *knew* I wasn't strong enough to propel my body far enough out to reach the key. I was watching players who were fitter, taller and more agile than me try, and fail. So if I couldn't do that – the actual purpose of the task – what was the point of the ocean faceplant? I did what can be instant gameplay death for many a *Survivor* player: I refused to even give it a go.

You haven't experienced humiliation until you've stood all alone on a platform, cameras rolling, while Jonathan LaPaglia narrates your despair. 'GEORGE – HE'S STUCK ON THE PLATFORM, HE DOESN'T WANT TO JUMP!' Yes, thank you JLP, we can all see what's happening.

Then comes humiliation squared: watching it all play out on TV a few months later, as every other *Survivor* fan screams at their televisions for you to JUST JUMP, GEORGE!

That moment was really the tipping point in the season, where my underperformance in challenges became a stick for my opponents to beat me with. It was raised consistently at tribal councils. At one in particular, I had to sit and listen as contestant Dani Beale – a challenge powerhouse herself – told the jury specifically about how physically weak I was, as they all nodded solemnly. None of them had watched *Survivor* before, and they wouldn't value the incredible political and social game they'd see before them because they didn't have a measure to place against it.

I *was* underperforming in physical challenges, and while I knew I was never going to be some thick-necked wall of muscle, I also knew there was room for improvement. This was a weakness that was visible for all to see – so I needed to work on it to claw back some power.

As soon as I was home from my first season, I started to prepare for my *Survivor* return. Now, I didn't actually *know* that I was heading back for another season of the show – but I also knew that if I left it until I got the call to start preparing my body, it'd be too late. I figured I'd made enough of a splash in my first season that it could be a possibility, so preparations started immediately.

And I do mean immediately. I literally got off the plane from Cloncurry, dumped my luggage at home, and headed to an F45 class. I hate going to the gym – there are about 100 other things I'd prefer to do in my spare time, like play a poker game or hang out at the pub with Mike and Stevie – but having just filmed a season being known as a challenge flop was a great motivator. I kept at it, going back to my learned habit of daily gym classes (as well as picking up every unknown number that buzzed my phone).

As expected, about seven months later, I got that call inviting me to return to the game. You'd think I wouldn't be as excited the second time around, but I really was. Another opportunity to play the game I loved so much? Sign me up.

I found out a few details in that first call, including that I would be cast as a 'villain' for the season (from 'Brains' to 'Villains'? Seemed like an upgrade to me), and the happiest news of all: with borders open, filming would return to tropical Samoa.

I had felt at home in Outback Cloncurry. I enjoyed the touch of the fine red dust on my hands, the stars shining as bright as I'd ever seen, the knowledge that the nearest capitol city was 2000 kilometres away, and the constant threat of brown snakes keeping my adrenaline levels high for 47 days. But Samoa? This was what I wanted out of *Survivor*: ocean swims, white sandy beaches, coconut feasts. Finally, the full *Survivor* experience.

As my second season approached, I realised my fitness regime just wasn't cutting it. That kind of workout was great for sedentary office workers to keep their waistlines slim, but not as helpful for more advanced fitness goals. I knew I needed to put on muscle – and functional muscle, not just bodybuilder toyboy muscle.

So around four months before the show started filming, King George went full Schwarzenegger.

I joined a local CrossFit gym and threw everything I had at the problem. For three months, I paid $545 a week (!) for a special, all-inclusive program that included daily personal training workouts and all my meals cooked for me. The gym was a sweaty, spartan warehouse space in Bankstown run by a super-fit husband and wife couple who made it their personal mission to get me as fit as they possibly could.

I spent hours and hours each week in that gym, exerting so much energy that on more than one occasion I had to sit down otherwise I might have thrown up. And what a waste that would've been, chucking up one of my ultra-expensive, home-cooked and macro-counted organic meals. So much of what I was eating was about replacing something delicious with something that, while it may have looked similar, tasted completely different. Zucchini spirals are NOT spaghetti. Shredded cauliflower is NOT rice. But I was firmly committed to my personal mission: *Survivor* is my Olympics and if I wanted to win gold, I needed to be stronger than I could have ever imagined.

Over those 12 weeks, I shredded down to 72 kilograms, became adept at an array of workouts of the day and body lifts, and was feeling and looking great. It was a far cry from when I was 95 kilos, couldn't do three push-ups and was drinking six energy drinks a day.

Did I enjoy the process? Absolutely not. Hours spent in the gym doing squats, thrusts and burpies, then going home to warm up high-protein, low carb, low fat meals? What a punish. But I knew what needed to be done to re-enter *Survivor* from a position of strength and banish any notion of weakness from my fellow players.

And it worked. Round two on *Survivor*, and I'd beaten the 'challenge weakling' allegations. I looked, felt and acted stronger – and I'd also gained much more confidence during my expensive workout regime, meaning there were no more 'choke' moments during challenges for my tribemates to stew over.

It's a hard-to-swallow truth about claiming your power:

SOMETIMES YOU HAVE TO HEAR THE CRITICISM, ACCEPT IT AND ACTUALLY WORK ON YOURSELF BEFORE YOU'LL BE ABLE TO GAIN THE UPPER HAND.

I could have just ignored all the naysayers chiding me for my limp athletic performance and trusted I could survive on my wits alone. But because I listened to people's complaints about me, I could take away *their* power and give it back to myself. I figured that if I could change those parts of me people didn't like, well, then they'd have nothing to complain about.

Now, those of you who watched my second season of *Survivor* might have a question here: *But George – didn't you faceplant in, like, the very first challenge? Really badly?*

Thanks for the reminder. But it's true: despite returning to *Survivor* as a stronger, more confident player, I suffered a pretty horrendous injury at the first hurdle that almost ended my game right then and there. After working so hard to be physically fit for the game, it wasn't my quads that nearly let me down – it was my head.

Day Two in the game, all still hyper on excitement and adrenaline, we were summoned to our first immunity challenge. It was an obstacle course with a very tricky start. Players had to hurl themselves, in pairs, onto one of two big boxes, which would then spin and fling them off the other side into a pit of mud.

This was my moment: the first physical challenge to show off to everyone – players and viewers alike – that this wasn't the soft-boiled George of the previous season. I wanted them to see what $545 a week of kangaroo patties and deadlifts looked like. That I had changed. That I was strong. That I would destroy people with my mind *and* my body.

So when it was my turn, I sprinted as fast as I could at the box, throwing myself onto it with velocity. My body landed on it with a thud as my tribemates spun it so that I'd be catapulted off the other side.

It was all going so fast: the running, the spinning, the yelling. Before I knew it, I landed headfirst, at speed, into the mud pit underneath the box.

I saw stars. Thick, muddy water coated my face. My recollection was that I dragged myself to the edge of the mud pool, at which point I could feel my neck was in pain. Jonathan could see it had been a bad fall, so he screamed the single word you never want to hear on *Survivor*: 'MEDIC!'

Hearing that word in reference to yourself is every *Survivor* player's worst nightmare. It could literally be the end of your game. My neck was throbbing, I couldn't see, and before I knew it I was in a neck-brace and a Samoan ambulance being taken for an urgent assessment. If you need to leave the game to receive medical attention, your window as a *Survivor* player starts to rapidly close. First, a stopwatch is started: you can only have 24 hours out of the game before you're disqualified. And that's if you are even allowed back in: they can't send a sick or injured player back into the game, and oftentimes people never come back from the tent.

I can only recall a few things from that accident. Firstly, I asked to be taken off the stretcher to finish the challenge (which production, of course, refused). When the senior members of the crew voiced their concerns, I then started to worry that my neck was broken. And I remember tearing up as I was being accompanied by a doctor on the 90-minute drive to the main hospital in Apia, Samoa.

It was only when the ambulance eventually arrived at the hospital that I realised there was someone laid out next to me in the emergency department: Jackie Glazer, a fellow returning player and professional poker player. I had met Jackie 10 years earlier at a poker game at Revesby Workers Club, and about six weeks before leaving for Samoa, I had played in Jackie's signature Jackstar Australian Poker League series, coming second and winning $22,000. Jackie *probably* knew she was going to be on *Survivor* again at that stage, and she *probably* suspected I would be too, and that we would *probably* be on the same Villains tribe. But neither one of us said a word. (Poker players are good like that – we can keep our cards close to our chest.) Playing with her in Samoa felt like finding an ace up my sleeve. But now the odds felt impossibly stacked against us.

'George, it's me,' she rasped. Her voice was so close, but I couldn't turn to look at her because I was immobilised in the neck brace.

It turns out that Jackie and I were injured at the same time during the challenge. I hadn't realised she was also in trouble – I couldn't see after falling head first into that mud pit, and then I was laid out on the ground, put in a neck brace and told not to move. All the while I was wondering if I had a spinal cord injury, I assumed she'd already sprinted off to the next obstacle.

But here she was with me, the two of us having bounced off to hospital on the backroads of Samoa, every pothole sending shivers of pain through our aching bodies.

Despite the little resources that Samoan nurses work with, I felt like I was in a safe pair of hands in the Apia hospital. Jackie and I were given fentanyl – a definite first for me – while we waited for our X-rays. I remember it making me feel happy and giddy despite the circumstances. As the night ticked along, Jackie and I kept ourselves distracted by telling each other stories about getting into the game. It helped take our minds off things (and I'm sure the hardcore painkillers didn't hurt, either).

At one point, we could hear a conversation between the Samoan doctor and the doctor from production. They said:

'The male patient has to be admitted. I suspect he has fractured his neck. The female patient can't be admitted as we don't have the expertise to treat her in Samoa. She has to be sent home.'

Jackie and I immediately started crying. They believed I had broken my neck. My thoughts about returning to the game moved to fretting about what the recovery process was for a fractured vertebrae.

Jackie's injury was so severe that she had to be sent to a bigger hospital. It sounded like we were both out of the game.

It was one of the lowest points of my life. Jackie was wheeled off, and I was left in the hospital room alone. I was told that I would need to have an MRI scan to confirm the fracture. In Australia, sometimes it can take weeks to book in an MRI scan. But in Samoa, there is *one* qualified radiologist and *one* MRI machine. Even more unluckily, most people do not work in Samoa on a Sunday, and it was late on Sunday night heading into the wee hours of Monday morning.

What kept my spirits up at the time was the fact that the *Survivor* production team looked after me to the best of their abilities with the resources available. I even was given the local spiritual treatment: in the middle of the night, as the hours were ticking by on my 24-hour deadline, the local Samoan fixer was by my bedside literally praying for me. She kept telling me that the doctors in the hospital were her nieces and nephews, and that I would have my MRI scan.

At about 3am, the *one* radiologist on the island came to

my bedside and told me I was being taken to the MRI room. After the prayers, this felt like a miracle. What I didn't know then was that the Samoan Health Minister had received a call from the fixer and demanded that the radiologist front up to the hospital to do my scan.

I remember my emotions during the MRI so clearly: I was torn between being worried about my ability to walk back into my camp, and my ability to walk properly again at all. I obviously didn't want my neck to be broken, but at the same time, I couldn't stop focusing on the fact that the very narrow window of opportunity to re-enter the game was closing.

They had told me if there was no fracture, they could consider sending me back to camp. So when the scan ended, I basically yelled to the radiologist, 'TELL ME NOW IF IT'S BROKEN.'

His words were to the point: 'Not that I can see, but there is significant swelling.'

This was music to my ears, which I had become very aware of while immobile in my neck brace. I had to wait another five hours for the scan to be reviewed by doctors in Australia. At around 8am I was given the good news: no break or fracture, just significant swelling. I demanded the neck brace to be taken off and for me to be taken back to camp *immediately*.

The doctors had other ideas. I was advised to sit upright in my bed for 30 minutes because I had been immobilised horizontally for about 21 hours at that stage. Finally, when I got up on my feet, I still had limited mobility in my neck movements. My right shoulder was not feeling good, but I was able to walk to the bathroom.

It was then that I saw myself in the mirror for the first time and burst into laughter. My forehead was still bloody and muddy and I looked like I had been badly beaten up outside the local bar. But the Samoan fixer's prayers had seemingly worked, and before I knew it, I was discharged and being driven back to the Villains camp.

But I still wasn't in the total clear to re-enter the game. I had to have a serious chat with the Executive Producer and the psychologist at their production camp. Clearly it would have been their worst nightmare to have two medical evacuations from the game, on the same day, so early in the season.

The psychologist did an assessment of me. He was worried about my emotional trauma. I was worried about having lost 23 hours in the game to work the numbers.

'There's no medical basis to not let me return,' I said to him bluntly. 'I am going back in – rain, hail or shine.'

They gave in. I was cleared. I asked for my Buff and backpack, ate an apple that was on the table – my first meal in three days – and told them both that it would look good on camera for me to return bloodied and bruised. I was ready.

I was driven a bit closer to camp and remember walking down the path while telling myself that I was lucky. Lucky my injury was not as bad as Jackie's, lucky that my dream was still alive, and lucky that all of the energy, time and money I had put into getting my body stronger for the game might have been the difference between being able to return and being flown back to Australia in that neck brace.

When I got back into camp, everybody was happy to have me back except for Michael and Simon, who seemed happy I wasn't seriously injured, but annoyed that I returned. The tribe couldn't stop talking about how bloodied, battered and bruised I was. Shonee, Liz, and Stevey insisted on trying to wash me in the sea water; for me this was literally like my baptism back into the game, ahead of my resurrection.

I knew I was in trouble from a strategy perspective. My closest ally Jackie was flying home to learn her fate, and my other close ally Anjali Rao had been voted off. (I knew Anjali from her time as a *Dateline* journalist on SBS rather than her infamous appearance on *Real Housewives of Melbourne*, which she loved about me.) I may not have been able to turn my neck for a few days, but my feet and mind were fine, and I hit the ground running to re-affirm the support of my tribemates, particularly Liz and Shonee. If I had Liz and Shonee backing me, I would survive the next couple of votes, and I may have lost time in the game to build bonds, but I knew I had it in me to make up lost ground.

The greatest risk in the game for me at that stage was infection thanks to the healing hole in the middle of my forehead. I was being pumped with antibiotics and told to somehow 'keep it clean'. I would ask my tribemates everyday how my scar was looking, and they would inspect it and hesitantly say 'better'. Thank God there were no mirrors, otherwise I probably would've spent most of my downtime in the game looking at that thing in the mirror and picking at it.

My face scar never went away after the game. Eventually I visited a cosmetic dermatologist, explained how it happened, and he diagnosed it as a traumatic tattoo – essentially the mud tattooed my forehead during the impact on the ground. It seems I'd hit the mud so hard, ripping my skin in the process, that the mud had imprinted itself into the underlayer of my skin like a tattoo. No amount of sea-water baths would remove it.

The pain from my injuries lingered through the season, but I didn't let the trauma stick around and rule my game. The worst had already happened, so it allowed me to approach my strategy with a no-holds-barred attitude. There's nothing like a near-death experience to put things into perspective (and I do mean 'near-death'; our spinal cords are delicate things). For me, it added an extra layer of motivation to throw everything I had at the game and win. Glory or Death in the most literal sense!

My faceplant didn't ruin the rest of my time on *Survivor* — in fact, it might have benefited me.

I WORE MY MUD TATTOO LIKE A BADGE OF HONOUR: KING GEORGE, WEAK IN CHALLENGES? TAKE A LOOK AT THIS!

The day after I returned, I relied on my much improved quad strength to help the tribe on a pushing-related log challenge. The squats and CrossFit had paid off. I had a physical representation of how tough and dedicated I was imprinted on my forehead. Every time someone spoke to me and to my bloody lump, they'd know I was all in. (Plus, nothing scares people just a little like a dark, gruesome wound on full display.)

There were four months between finishing filming in Samoa and Episode One going to air, which meant four months of me being unable to explain my newfound face tat to my friends, family and people coming up to me on the street. People would always tell me I had makeup on my face, thinking the dark smudge was some foundation gone wrong. I would say 'Rub it off, quick!' and then pretend to be disappointed when they couldn't.

Nowadays, I'm not in constant training, waiting for the inevitable call from the *Survivor* execs. I'm no longer living life like I could be called upon at short notice to go up against athletes and bodybuilders in punishing endurance challenges ... but I *have* made a promise to my bodybuilder *Survivor* frenemy Simon Mee that when I return for my sixth season, I will have more muscles than he had in Samoa.

I learned a valuable lesson during my preparation health kick: there's no shame in listening to criticism and using it as fuel to better yourself. If your enemies are hurling insults at you, listen to them and work out what you might be able to use to your advantage. One of the best ways to disarm the opposition is to take away their ammunition – and turn your biceps into weapons instead.

And those healthy habits have stuck around. While at first I was working hard on my body to have better odds at *Survivor*, now I keep on working out to have better odds in life. For the first time, I've kept up my fitness for a sustained period of time. It was an important realisation. If I'm going to put all that effort in for a few weeks spent playing a game on a tropical island, why not put the effort in during the rest of my life, too?

Besides, who knows – my friends in the reality-TV world all have my phone number. They know who to call if they need some spice on the screen.

ONE OF THE BEST WAYS TO DISARM THE OPPOSITION IS TO TAKE AWAY THEIR AMMUNITION – AND TURN YOUR BICEPS INTO WEAPONS INSTEAD.

FIGURE OUT WHAT PEOPLE WANT – THEN GIVE IT TO THEM

I had a lightbulb moment while filming a confessional in my first season of *Survivor* that changed not how I played the game, but how I *talked* about playing it.

History is famously written by the victorious, but in the land of television, it's spoken by the loudest.

Confessionals are the scenes that pepper every *Survivor* episode where players sit away from camp in some picturesque spot and spout pithy soundbites about what's going on in the game. They're also quite the point of contention when seasons air – some players barely get a look in, while others seem to end up narrating the whole season.

My first confessional was filmed before we were even on location. It was with a producer in Sydney Town Hall before we were flown into the Outback. Credit where credit is due, I was lucky to be surrounded by world class, experienced producers on *Australian Survivor*. The role of a story producer is simple on a reality-TV show: they help shape a narrative around the content created by contestants.

While it was my first time appearing on a TV show, I knew that I had to make each producer's job easy by giving interesting answers about my thought processes on the game, or in my commentary of what was happening around me. I knew this because preparing my boss for television and radio appearances was a basic function of my job when I worked for the Member for Bankstown.

I would prepare options for lines she could use in both interviews and press releases that offered different perspectives, all emphasising different points. What she taught me was that in any kind of TV media, quality always measured over quantity. For example, after a 10 minute interview with a news journalist, only 10 words would often make the final news edit. Every word has to be punchy and to the point, otherwise the news editors would simply use a snappier option from another politician.

I took what I'd learned managing the press pool and applied it to TV.

IF YOU CONTROL YOUR SOUND BITES, YOU CONTROL THE EDITORS AND YOU THEREFORE CONTROL THE NARRATIVE.

But I couldn't just spout out whatever wisdom I liked. I knew the editors were looking for specific grabs that they could use to illustrate what was going in the game. Just like the journalists want to put the punchiest politicians on the 5pm news, if I could give a more salacious answer than any other contestant, then I'd get more confessional time, and the audience gets more King George.

This realisation happened about halfway through Brains v Brawn. At that point in filming, I was feeling comfortable in front of camera and knew I would be a key narrator of the season for two reasons: a) I was involved in every aspect of gameplay; and b) I was giving stimulating commentary on what was happening around me.

One day I settled on to my usual rock to talk about what was going on back at camp. I was asked a question about something going on in the game that day, and I gave my answer. They called 'Cut', and went to move on to another topic. Then I said, 'Stop – I'm not done.'

I gave an answer to the same question from a different perspective, setting up a different situation that I could deliver on back in camp. They nodded and went on with the next question. Again, I said, 'No, I'm not done. I'm gonna give you one more grab.' I wanted to give them another option for a soundbite to use, just in case the game moved in another direction based on plans I was contemplating but hadn't enacted yet. This was good for me, because no matter what I chose to do back in the reality of the game, this meant that they'd have a good snippet from me they could insert into the action to explain what was happening.

I was feeling chuffed with myself. I remember a warm rush through my body – no doubt heightened by the hunger and the tiredness – as I thought to myself: George, I think you might be nailing this game.

I kept that up throughout my time on *Survivor*, insisting on giving a few options with each confessional to make sure they had a stable of soundbites available when they were putting the edit of the show together. I'd make one cheeky, another really fiery. In one I'd be dismayed by a fellow player's move, in another I'd laugh about it. And I noticed a very clear trend start to occur: I was being ushered off to film a lot more confessionals than most of my fellow players. Some would go days without the call to go and spill their secrets on camera away from camp; I was lapping them as the producers returned to me time and time again. I was starting to feel like David Attenborough: *Australian Survivor*, narrated by King George.

Here's the thing: some people go onto reality TV for fame or fortune, but 99 per cent of these people will not experience them, because they either don't have any talent or do not come across as being very interesting. Obviously that big cash prize should also be a goal, but you could make that sort of money by investing wisely in the share market or flipping properties. If you're on a reality-TV show, you want your story to be told on-air and then to seize all the opportunities that may present themselves after you've lodged yourself in the public's consciousness. *That* should be your number-one goal as a contestant.

And that means you need airtime. What I knew as a TV newbie was that I was more likely to make an impact in the game if I was an active player, and this would lead to a lot of confessionals on the show. Can you imagine telling your loved ones you're on *Survivor*, settling in to watch the show with them, and episode after episode, just seeing the back of your head in crowd shots as other, more interesting players get all the screentime? I was not going to let that embarrassing situation happen to me, and I adjusted my actions in the game accordingly.

I applied a three-step process that you can extend to most power-holders:

1. identify what they need and want (engaging confessionals);
2. deliver it by the bucketload (giving them several good options each time);
3. and then they respond positively (turning me into the King of Confessionals).

You can follow these instructions to get a lot of what you want out of life – and by helping someone *else* get what they want. Instead of pouring all of your energy into advancing your own goals, sometimes assisting other people with getting closer to achieving theirs is the best way to stay in their good graces.

It's a simple method to getting ahead that I'd honed in my previous job. Being a political operator is all about figuring out what your bosses want and need, and delivering it for them. My old boss in politics, Tania Mihailuk, was at the time the Shadow Minister in charge of the fair-trading portfolio. It's about as boring as it sounds: a low-profile portfolio, dealing with a lot of business rules, industry groups and regulations. It's a decidedly unglamorous gig for any politician tasked with looking after it; very few big photo ops or attention-grabbing media stories arise from it.

I knew my boss wanted to change that and make some waves, so I was always on the lookout for an opportunity to help her do it. Tania worked hard at her job, because a hard-working MP shines in front of their colleagues, media and the industry. As a newly elected MP and first-time Shadow Minister, this was an opportunity for her to establish her credentials in the Shadow Cabinet.

I found our chance to generate a hurrah when I spotted a little, low-interest proposal to change painters' licensing requirements. The proposal had come from the government at the time, and if passed, it would've meant that you

INSTEAD OF POURING ALL OF YOUR ENERGY INTO ADVANCING YOUR OWN GOALS, SOMETIMES ASSISTING OTHER PEOPLE WITH GETTING CLOSER TO ACHIEVING THEIRS IS THE BEST WAY TO STAY IN THEIR GOOD GRACES.

wouldn't need to do a TAFE course to become a licensed painter of homes and the like. You could just 'be' a painter, no qualification needed.

Immediately, I saw an opportunity in us opposing the proposal. If spun correctly, this unassuming project could become a hot-button issue, and could be a way to help my boss achieve her personal goal of being a tireless defender of industry, standing up to the government.

Those proposing the changes no doubt hoped they wouldn't provoke the ire of Big Business. But I wanted all eyes on us, so I made sure they knew. The Master Painters Association of NSW were understandably outraged when I alerted them to the proposal. They *hated* it: it would deregulate their industry, meaning all those hours and dollars their painter members spent getting their accreditation had essentially been a waste of time and money.

And what about everyday people? Well, there are always two sides to a story. The Minister championing the proposal said that removing the red tape of the licensing requirements would bring down costs, meaning you could hire someone (with less qualifications) to paint your house at a cheaper rate. But we argued that would lead to worse quality work in the industry, as well as angry painters (ie voters) who would be undercut by unqualified painters. Surely people would rather pay a little extra for a job well done than a half-baked job from an Irish backpacker painting your living room before their visa runs out?

With the Master Painters Association on board and with our messaging to the public locked in, we hit the road. We went on a full media blitz, hitting up local papers in every single corner of NSW with a sexy story to sell them: the State Government is trying to screw over skilled, hardworking tradies. You can already see the headlines, complete with photos of angry-looking painters, arms folded with paint brushes in hand, can't you?

My boss had wanted an attention-grabbing issue, and I'd delivered, all from a low-interest proposal that could've easily been waved through without a second thought. This was at the start of my career as a political advisor, and Tania never forgot that. By controlling the narrative and getting her what she wanted, I earned her respect and won both of us credibility.

DELIVERING RESULTS IS SOMETIMES THE BEST WAY TO MAKE FRIENDS AND POSITIVELY INFLUENCE PEOPLE IN A PROFESSIONAL SETTING.

I'd identified what my boss wanted from me, and I delivered it. Whether it's some media attention for your supervisor or a soundbite for your producers, find out what people want from you, and give it to them. It's a sure-fire way to collect allies and build your base.

CHAPTER 7

GET OUT OF YOUR COMFORT ZONE

If your aim is to win friends, it's important you cast your net wide.

NEW FRIENDS COME FROM NEW EXPERIENCES – THE MORE, THE BETTER.

There are almost 8 billion people in the world, which means there are important, lasting connections up for grabs every time you leave the house. But that's the key: you have to actually get out of your comfort zone in the first place to make them.

Take perhaps one of the most impulsive decisions I've ever made. It was May 2019, and I was about 18 months into a stint working in government policy, feeling bored of the daily grind and eager for more excitement in the routine of my public sector nine to five.

Any office worker knows the feeling, and it usually gets worse as the weather gets colder and the days get shorter: up before sunrise, trudging into the office on public transport, eight hours of work before you trudge back home just as the sun is setting and the evening chill is setting in. Some days, the most exciting thing you'll do is try a new flavour of muffin at your local cafe.

My time working in politics was intense, but the pressure of the job kept me fired up and revving. I left for the public sector in 2017 at the top of my game, with the feeling that I didn't have anything more to achieve as a staff member while we were in Opposition. Compared to my cut-throat years as a political operative, my career in the public sector was very different: this job was all about wading through bureaucracy and paper-pushing.

Needing a little distraction while I was at my desk, I clicked on a news story about Australia's entry for the Eurovision Song Contest taking place the following week in Tel Aviv, Israel.

Ah, Eurovision. Where do I begin to describe my lifelong love affair with this sequined singing spectacular? It's the world's largest televised singing competition, with countries from across Europe sending their best musical act each year to perform a three-minute song. Past Eurovision winners include ABBA, Celine Dion and a Finnish death-metal band called Lordi who performed wearing terrifying latex monster masks. I know, disturbing, isn't it? Celine Dion's *Canadian*.

With our huge population of European migrants, Australia's always had a mad fascination with the contest – and in 2015, we were rewarded for our fervour with an invitation to compete.

What's that you say? Australia isn't part of Europe? Australia has been a home to some of the highest populations of migrants from Europe for over 100 years, and geopolitically, based on our Eurovision voting record, we are considered as an honourary member of the Scandi voting block. I personally welcome our Swedish and Danish overlords.

That year, we were sending the quirky pop-opera singer–songwriter Kate Miller-Heidke to the competition with the song 'Zero Gravity'. It was a spectacular performance (which ended up only placing ninth in the competition – robbed!).

Slumped at my desk, one eye out for managers wondering what I was doing, I watched rehearsal footage of Miller-Heidke and her back-up dancers. They were balanced atop giant wobbling stilts, and she never missed a note as she veered this way and that. Gasping every time one of them teetered from side to side, I realised this was exactly the sort of excitement I'd been missing from life lately.

I wasn't about to take up stilt-walking, but I was down to hurtle through the sky in a giant flying metal tube. I pulled up some travel websites and did some hasty research. Half an hour later, I was knocking on the door of my Executive Director's office.

'Would you mind if I took a bit of leave soon for a holiday – say, 10 days?'

'That should be fine, George,' she muttered, barely looking up from her computer. 'When are you thinking?'

'In three days.'

That got her attention.

I knew she wouldn't exactly be thrilled, so I came prepared: I'd checked that nobody else on my team would be on leave for the next couple of weeks, and I knew we had no important deadlines or projects looming (hence the office ennui). I explained I'd stay across emails and check in when I needed to, making it as easy as possible for her to say yes. She relented, saying she'd approve the leave – I think in part just to get me to stop pestering her.

I raced back to my desk and started booking my flights, my heart racing as I thought about everything I'd need to organise within the next couple of days. I'm not usually one for grand impulsive gestures – I prefer to weigh my options before making an informed decision about how to proceed – but sometimes in life, you just have to go for it. This was one of those moments: my heart was telling me to go and explore the world, so I listened.

So there I was, only three days later, boarding a flight from Sydney to Tel Aviv – via Addis Ababa, Ethiopia. The Ethiopia detour wasn't actually because of the last-minute booking: I'd actively looked for a stopover that would give my brain a much-needed hit of the unknown. I'd spent 18 months in a bland job staring at my computer screen for 35 hours a week – give me something different!

And different is certainly what I got. I booked my flights separately so I could spend a little time in Addis Ababa, about 40 hours all up. Just a few days after having my little office existential crisis about how mundane my life was, here I was, spat out into an African metropolis.

I'M NOT USUALLY ONE
FOR GRAND IMPULSIVE
GESTURES, BUT
SOMETIMES IN LIFE,
YOU JUST HAVE TO
GO FOR IT.

I'd arrived in the hottest month of the year – excellent planning, George – and the air was sticky and thin because Addis Ababa is at an elevation higher than the highest point in Australia. I was ripe with excitement as my taxi from the airport weaved through street markets and traffic jams to take me to my hotel. Addis Ababa was peak intrigue for me. It was my first time to Africa, and the most 'exotic' country this Western Sydney boy had visited previously was Vietnam. I enjoy hustle and bustle, but to see it firsthand in a vibrant city like Addis was exhilarating for me.

I only gave myself half an hour in my hotel room to shower and change before forcing myself back out onto the city streets to explore. This is what I came for: King George does Africa. Time to get amongst it.

Thankfully, I wasn't completely adrift in this foreign land. I'd booked a tour guide before I flew in, and he treated me well, shepherding me through the bustling city of more than five million people safely. He also took me out of the city, as we journeyed to the spectacular Blue Nile Gorge, 200 kilometres north of the city and considered Ethiopia's own Grand Canyon.

The tour was coming to an end on my second day in Ethiopia, and I was flying on to Tel Aviv late that night.

Not wanting to whittle away time at my hotel, I mentioned to my tour guide that I'd love to see some football. I was in luck: the Ethiopia Premier League had a game that very afternoon. The tour was meant to be over, but my guide was insistent: he'd take me to the game and watch with me.

And that's how I found myself as the only foreigner in a crowd of 35,000 supporters at Addis Ababa stadium. The adventure began outside, where all the people who couldn't get tickets set up colourful tents to eat, drink and at least listen to the game happening inside the stadium. Smoke filled the air as meat sizzled on portable BBQs. There was music, singing, dancing – it almost seemed a shame to have to leave the party and go inside the stadium.

I was treated like a King by the locals who were very excited to have an Australian join their pre-game festivities. Group after group would try to usher me into their tents, offering me Ethiopian beers and plates of food – including some raw meat I definitely wasn't going to risk trying.

The party atmosphere continued inside the stadium. The roar of the crowd was deafening, but there was a joy to it, too.

I'd been to countless football games by this point in my life, but this was something else. Everyone seated around me wanted to wave, smile and even sometimes get a selfie, apparently convinced that the one foreigner in the stadium must be a visiting celebrity. (They were ahead of the curve treating me like a star, seeing as this was about 14 months before my first season of *Survivor* aired.)

It wasn't all so wholesome, though. I remember at one point, a few local beers in, popping to the loo and being met with quite a ... *confronting* sight. And smell. Every horror story I'd heard about bathroom cleanliness while traveling overseas was suddenly right there in front of me. But weirdly, I wasn't too horrified as I held my nose and tried to pee as quickly as possible.

Just a few days earlier I'd been at my desk drowning in paperwork and counting down the hours until 5pm. Now I was using an open sewer as a public toilet in Ethiopia's national stadium.

THIS IS LIVING!

The high continued when I got to Tel Aviv (and, thankfully, the toilet hygiene standards were also higher). The city was in full Eurovision mode by the time I arrived. At 29, for the first time in my life, I was staying in a hostel. I immediately did a random interview for a German public broadcaster with a journalist who was staying in the bunk above. He told me I was a natural on camera ... this turned out to be good foreshadowing.

Tel Aviv is known as one of the great party towns of the world, but I didn't know that when I landed. I had done no research on the city beforehand, and the only time I had heard Israel mentioned in the media was in relation to the ongoing conflict over Palestine. I thought the people would be tense and on edge, but instead everybody was living their best lives. The locals would hop from the main beach to the amazing restaurants, cafes and bars dotting the alleyways a few streets behind.

Tel Aviv for me was like the Gold Coast on steroids, but with much friendlier people – all of whom seemed to have ripped bodies gained *without* steroids.

I ignored most of the usual tourist attractions in favour of going 'full Eurovision'. I wanted to immerse myself in the song contest I had, until this point, only ever watched on television. I was spoiled for choice. Eurovision isn't just that four-hour grand final that airs on SBS. There are also semi-finals, a Eurovision village, jury finals and my best discovery of the week, Euroclub: a huge dancefloor that only played Eurovision bangers until 6am, with amazing shawarma readily available around the corner. It was like finding heaven in the Holy Land.

It was such a last-minute trip, and tickets to those headline events had sold out months beforehand. It struck me only as

I was landing in Tel Aviv: would my impulsive Eurovision pilgrimage be worth my while, without a ticket to … anything? Or would I find myself tantalisingly close to the action, but still so far?

I hadn't given myself time to think in the past few days, but I was suddenly nervous I'd been a little *too* impulsive. I didn't want to end up watching the contest on Tel Aviv beach at Eurovillage, sad Aperol spritz in hand as I tried not to think about my bank balance.

Thankfully, the good thing about Eurovision is you actually don't need tickets to any of the official events to have a good time; usually, the best parties are happening elsewhere, in bars and free public spaces that get swarmed by Eurovision fans from around the globe. And when you find good people, you also manage to find grand final tickets … like I did.

I threw myself into the few days I had there, heading to bars by myself and introducing myself to fellow Eurovision tragics. The common interest was already there, so conversations flowed freely. Some were one-night friends, just a smiling face to stand with at the bar and debate which countries should make it through to the semi-finals. But others developed into more lasting friendships.

For example, I struck up a real friendship in my time in Tel Aviv with a Labor hack from South Australia, my friend Simone. At a meet-up of travelling Aussies, we were all talking about the 2019 Federal Election that was being held at the same time as the Eurovision final. We all knew which vote Australia cared more about.

After realising we were both involved in the Labor Party in different ways, Simone and I did a token 30 minutes of handing out fliers at a pre-poll at the Australian Embassy in Tel Aviv. (Nobody can say we didn't help during the election.) From there, we mingled with a melting pot of fans from throughout the world. Helpfully, most people usually displayed their national pride, wrapping themselves in national flags and dressing in their country's colours.

In one week in Tel Aviv, I met more new people – and made more new friendships – than I had in a year back home, stuck in my little work/sleep/repeat rut. I'd pushed myself out of my comfort zone, boosted my confidence and it was paying off in spades (even if my credit card would take some time to pay off).

The friendship with Simone has stayed and we travelled together to the 2023 Eurovision in Liverpool. I have an open offer of a month's free accommodation in Oslo thanks to a

Norwegian couple I met in a market alley. This is handy, because in 2024, Eurovision heads to Sweden, so I plan to visit via Norway and take them up on that offer. Likewise, I know there's a certain Ethiopian tour guide with a generous spirit who would happily put me up for a night or two should I ever find myself in Addis Ababa again.

I returned from my impulsive Eurovision trip with a new excitement about life. I'd shaken myself out of my rut, gained a new group of like-minded friends from around the world and reminded myself about the importance of following my passions in life.

YOU DON'T NEED TO TRAVEL TO EUROVISION OR ETHIOPIA TO FIND YOUR TRIBE, BUT YOU DO NEED TO PUSH YOURSELF.

Look at your interests and pursue them. Join a social club, a community network, even a Facebook page, and friendships can easily follow.

Don't be afraid to cultivate different, separate circles of friends for different interests. Too many people stick

THINK OF FRIENDSHIP
LIKE THE STOCK MARKET:
YOU WANT A DIVERSE
PORTFOLIO, ALL BRINGING
YOU VALUE IN THEIR
OWN WAY.

to one small circle of friends, say, their high school, uni or work contacts. My football mates are different to my poker player friends; my *Survivor* fam don't know my political buddies. Think of friendship like the stock market: you want a diverse portfolio, all bringing you value in their own way.

And if you want to diversify your portfolio, that means diversifying your experiences. Nobody makes gains on the market – be it stocks or friends – by playing it safe.

PART 2

MANIPULATING PEOPLE

GETTING YOUR FRIENDS TO BEND TO YOUR WILL

CHAPTER 8

BEND BUT DON'T BREAK THE RULES

It was the day before my first season of *Survivor* was due to start filming. I was waiting nervously, by myself, in a drab Outback motel room. Because of the pandemic, filming had moved from the usual locale of a beach in Fiji or Samoa to the Australian Outback: hot, dry and dusty Cloncurry, about an hour east of Mount Isa in middle-of-nowhere rural Queensland. And I mean middle of nowhere: Darwin was 17 hours' drive to the northwest and Brisbane 19 hours to the southeast.

I was isolated in a tiny, old room for several days at the Wagon Wheel Motel in Cloncurry – standard practice before reality-TV contestants enter a show. I think they like to make sure you're feeling really bored and lonely before they put a camera in your face, just so you're eager to give them good content.

My only company for most of the time were the truckers who'd congregate at a table right outside my window to chain-smoke through the day. Not that I was permitted to talk to them, though; I'd just eavesdrop on their rough-as-guts conversations about life on the road instead. Over the days I found myself getting emotionally involved. *Keith's got to get this cargo to Cairns by tomorrow morning*, I'd think. *He'd better finish his Four'N Twenty and hit the road.*

The season's players were assembled in just about every available motel room in town as we awaited the day we would head deeper into the Outback and start the game. Here's another brutal fact about reality TV: most reality shows usually string along a few 'alternates' until the moment the first camera starts recording, just in case a player drops out at the last minute. The alternates often don't find out their placeholder purpose until the *real* players are summoned – and they stay behind, trudging back to their normal, dreary lives shortly after.

There I was, sat in my poky little prison, privately fretting about whether I was an alternate, unable to even leave the room to go for a walk without a crew member chaperoning me to make sure my allotted sunlight break didn't clash with that of any of the other contestants. I was scheming, looking for any possible way to stand out from the pack. How could I guarantee that I'd be jumping into one of those Land Cruisers heading to camp tomorrow?

A producer stopped by my room to give me a pep talk. She asked me if I had any big plans for my time in the game.

Suddenly, my mood lifted. I'd been telling myself to keep to a boring but sensible game plan: don't look for idols too early. Don't be controversial. Keep your head down – at least in the initial part of the game, when anyone playing hard puts a target on their own back. But hearing that question, it was like a switch flipped and every *Survivor* fan dream I'd ever had came tumbling out.

'I'm going to do EVERYTHING,' I told her. 'Everything! I'm going to look for idols the moment I get there. I'm going to make strong alliances, oust my enemies, plot big blindsides … I'm going to do it *all*.'

She had an excited look on her face. I knew from that smirk that she thought she'd just hit reality-TV-contestant paydirt. In that moment, I knew I wasn't an alternate.

She reacted that way because if you want to succeed on a reality-TV show, you need to be a risk taker. There's nothing people hate more – and by 'people' I mean basically everyone involved with the sausage making that is reality TV, plus the viewers who eat it – than a contestant who's not willing to do anything once they get there. That happens on *Survivor*: people talk a big game on their audition tape, promise they're going to pull all sorts of moves and then just don't once they're out there.

I was suddenly feeling gutsy again, so I thought I would start to test my luck in this game: right here and right now, at the Wagon Wheel Motel, to see what I could get away with.

She asked me if I had any questions about the rules of the game, and I had one: *Survivor*'s 'one camera rule'. This is a common rule in reality TV: there are usually multiple cameras filming what happens, but when there is only one camera present – like late at night or when the other camera crew is off filming a confessional – you cannot do anything prime-time-worthy unless it's trained on you.

Now, I am a trained lawyer, despite never practising. I paid $60,000, studied for five years and completed my additional training at the College of Law to sign the lawyer's scroll at the Supreme Court of NSW. My strongest skills when I was training were always to do with statutory interpretation, namely:

WORK OUT HOW RULES ARE APPLIED IN LAYMAN'S TERMS, FIND LOOPHOLES AND WORK OUT HOW TO GET AROUND THEM.

Think of it like completing your annual tax return: tax laws are complex and intimidating, but the people who know how to navigate those rules pay less tax than others. It's not illegal for them to earn more money than their neighbour – they've just made the system work for them.

When I asked about the application of the standard one-camera rule, I got the generic explanation: if the camera's not on you, then you should avoid doing anything important until it's free, otherwise it won't be captured for the audience.

In other words, when you are sitting in camp and the sole camera person is over by the well, filming an intense heart-to-heart between two other contestants – by all means, go and pee in the bushes, wash the rice pot, or catch up on a nap. But don't hunt for an idol or start plotting a massive blindside, because that's potentially great TV that won't be captured by a camera.

Always one to challenge the rules, I had questions about this. What would happen if I stomped purposefully into the bush in the direction of an idol while the camera *wasn't* on me? Would production quickly scramble to make sure I was being filmed? Even if I didn't know an idol was that way, and I was just going for a pee?

Only, I didn't ask those questions out loud. Rather than announcing it, I kept quiet and decided to test it for myself once I was actually in the game.

The Australian Outback is open, vast and sparse. Filming *Survivor* in Samoa, the jungle was so dense behind the beach that you couldn't venture off the paths around camp and to the well. But in the Outback, you could wander in any direction you liked because the gum trees were spread out far apart. That means there were thousands of places idols could be hidden, and I was committed to finding one.

I was like a velociraptor in Jurassic Park, testing the fences for weaknesses. Wander out past this boulder across the riverbank, and no camera crew follows? OK, nothing there. Walk in the area covered by gumtrees behind the shelter with no company? No film team means it must be a no-go zone.

But I had noticed on Day One of the game that every single time a player went to the well, in a group or alone, they were followed by a camera. My instinct was saying that in this vast camp of what seemed like three to four square kilometres, the well seemed to be 'hot' with early game action. The obvious place for spicy conversations is the area near the well, so players who head there always have a camera with them, to capture B-roll footage or an important game-breaking conversation. But to follow them even when they were alone? That felt like overkill, especially on the first day of the game, when there were so many conversations to record.

NOT EVERYONE SEEMED TO GRASP THE MOST BASIC REALITY-TV RULE: THAT IF IT DOESN'T HAPPEN ON CAMERA, IT DOESN'T HAPPEN.

One night, I overheard members of the opposing alliance whispering at camp about who they wanted to vote out next: me. There was no camera in sight, so no vision was captured. Sure, I was annoyed to hear my name was on the chopping block, but the *Survivor* fan in me was also annoyed at their lousy gameplay. Plotting a big move? Guys, do it on camera! These are the same people who would then complain that they were not getting a fair edit in terms of screen time when the episode went to air.

So late on the first day in camp, I decided to venture to the well alone, yet again, and made sure that a cameraman was following.

I was more than happy to go on the one-kilometre walk to the well in 50°C heat, over and over, because it gave me an opportunity to find what I was looking for. And that's exactly what happened: next to the well was a white rock, seemingly out of place. Almost every Brains tribe member would have seen that rock during their conversations, but I was the first to flip it over, and dig around what seemed like a small white piece of thread that was partially exposed. I stumbled upon the Safety Without Power advantage, which would allow me to leave a tribal council early to save myself (though I couldn't cast a vote). It was an advantage that I detonated at the first tribal council the day after – one I wouldn't have had if I hadn't decided to use the rules of the game and apply them to my advantage.

All 24 *Survivor* players were handed the same set of rules. We were all provided the same briefing on what the rules meant. But I was the only person who decided to test their application. If you know the rules of the game better than your competition, then you can make them benefit you.

By Day Three, while most of my campmates were sunbaking by the dirty billabong, I was prowling around the vast campsite looking for anything I could find and having as many conversations as I could. On a reality-TV show, if you are doing something – like sunbathing – and the camera isn't recording it, then it is clearly the wrong thing to do.

This is why I found the hidden immunity idol now tattooed on my chest. (More on that later.) I had searched almost every single part of the camp with and without a camera crew, figuring out where the idol could possibly be through a process of elimination. Not in the north, not in the east, not by the well where I found my first advantage, perhaps across the billabong on the other side of camp? My then-not-mate Baden had been regularly going to the other side of the billabong, camera crew in tow. Baden had at that stage found a clue to the location of the idol, which I didn't know at the time. If Baden is looking there, I need to look there, I told myself. As it turned out, he just hadn't been looking hard enough.

These lessons also apply outside of *Survivor*, of course. I have always worked out ways to operate in the grey area,

IF YOU KNOW THE RULES OF THE GAME BETTER THAN YOUR COMPETITION, THEN YOU CAN MAKE THE RULES BENEFIT YOU.

finding legal loopholes that I could take advantage of. I honed this skill when I worked in politics, which is typically full of betrayal by operatives who often know how to bend their party's official 'rules'. These processes are publicly available on the Party's website and set out every internal procedure they have, from how to conduct a meeting to your eligibility to vote and running in Party ballots. It's long, it's boring and few people would ever bother to read it in full.

But of course I did. Two procedures stuck out to me: You had to attend two Party branch meetings a year to be an eligible voter in a Party ballot. You also had to renew your own membership. Not many people could be bothered doing either of these things, which meant that their membership – and our power as a collective – often lapsed. How could I get ensure the Party rules were followed to the tee while also making sure that supportive branch members didn't have their eligibility to vote expire unnecessarily?

The solution was simple. Aside from regular, boring, run of the mill meetings, I would always ensure that there would be a big Christmas Party branch meeting with free food and drinks for members who came, and then we'd always have a big February meeting to welcome in the New Year, with free-flowing membership renewal forms. Attend these two

YOU CAN AND MUST
PLAY ANY GAME FAIRLY,
BUT A THOROUGH
UNDERSTANDING OF HOW
TERMS AND CONDITIONS
ARE APPLIED CAN HELP
YOU SKEW THE ODDS
IN YOUR FAVOUR.

social, fun-filled meetings, and submit your forms online or in person, and you'd stay a voting member. This ticked the critical boxes of the Party rules and made sure that friendly branch members were always able to maintain a degree of control on the membership.

It's a great skill to master in life: making a situation work for you by bending but not breaking the rules. On *Survivor*, I never did anything without the cameras watching, as the rules stipulated – but I realised that following that very rule could lead me to the ultimate prize. In my political life, I always prioritised satisying administrative criteria at the same time as building the support of the decision-making Party members.

If you are given a set of rules, read them, become familiar with them and then use them to your advantage. You can and must play any game fairly, but a thorough understanding of how terms and conditions are applied can help you skew the odds in your favour. Do this correctly, and the only thing dissenters can complain about is not thinking of it themselves.

CHAPTER 9

GET YOUR WAY BY HELPING OTHER PEOPLE GET THEIRS

'Thank you, Macedonian Jesus!'

This proclamation became something of a catch phrase during my two seasons on *Survivor*. I'd declare it whenever the *Survivor* gods were smiling on me and my game was going well, and it stuck. In fact, google 'Macedonian Jesus' now and I'm the first entry. (Sorry, real Jesus.)

But it wasn't some cheesy line cooked up for reality TV. My appreciation for 'Macedonian Jesus' was born years earlier, when I secured a big win for the Macedonian Orthodox Church of New South Wales – and for myself.

'THANK YOU, MACEDONIAN JESUS!'

Churches are a little like businesses: in order to attract new clients, they need to update their offerings and bring their operations into the 21st century. Because God doesn't always help pay the bills, churches can apply for grants from the government to help them do this. Usually these are to pay for much-needed repairs and upgrades. Most places of worship were built a long time ago, and it can be prohibitively expensive for a church to suddenly put up a new roof, replace their pews or upgrade their sound system.

Some churches, like the Greek Orthodox Church in Bankstown, are all over this – they regularly apply for, and win, grants. Others, like the Macedonian Orthodox Church, don't even register. They're not politically inclined, have never had the right advice from parishioners internally and so have never asked for or received government handouts.

I decided I was going to do something about this and help out the Macedonian Orthodox churches in my local area, in nearby Cabramatta and Rosebery. Both definitely looked like they needed the cash injection of a government grant: both churches look spectacular on the inside, covered in Orthodox saints on stained glass windows, as well as murals and portraits. But on the outside, both could be described as not fit-for-purpose for their core parishioners, who were mostly elderly

Macedonian-Australians. The church in Cabramatta was not accessible, for example, with pensioners having to navigate multiple stairs. I will never forget my family friend Kiki Stojanoski, who uses an electronic wheelchair for mobility, being unable to enter to church in his wheelchair for his own mother's funeral. The church in Roseberry had a simpler problem: it was more accessible, but they wanted to improve the amenity of the church boundary with new fencing.

Having previously worked in a State MP's office, I knew that there were many different infrastructure-related grants available and that the first key step to obtaining funding was to put in a strong grant application. If there is one thing that I can do well (and there's a couple of them), it's identify what is wrong with something, find a solution and then tailor a grant application accordingly.

I know what you're thinking: What a good boy, George. Doing a good deed to help out the Macedonian Church! And that was certainly part of my motivation – but I'd be lying if I said that this was my *only* motivation.

Before I tell you what that was, let me tell you a little secret. I was helping out a church that I wasn't actually baptised into. I was baptised Greek Orthodox, not Macedonian Orthodox, which is a little fact I don't parade around to members of the local Macedonian community. I'm Macedonian on my dad's side, but I was baptised on my mum's Greek side.

If the old Macedonian men and women in the church just assume that George Mladenov is baptised Macedonian Orthodox, good for them – who am I to correct them? In truth, I'm agnostic. I ticked the box 'no religion' on my last census form.

I called the CEO of the Macedonian Orthodox Church here in New South Wales, the umbrella organisation that manages the affairs of the churches at Cabramatta and Roseberry, and we set up a meeting. I made my pitch, telling them they were missing out on government funding to improve the infrastructure at their churches and said that I'd like to help.

I explained the process and detailed what would help their grant application be successful: they'd need to prove their need to the local MP, and some demonstrable community outreach would also help, so they could show how important the church is to the local population. This meant it was time for the church to throw open its doors and engage with the local community in a more visible way.

I helped them schmooze in a way the local Macedonian church just hadn't done before. The Archbishop was visiting from Macedonia, and I helped organise a dinner so that a few local councillors and Members of Parliament could meet him. It was nothing fancy, just an opportunity for all those parties to break bread and get to know each other. The meeting got reported in the local Macedonian newspaper, establishing this new relationship. Suddenly, the Macedonian Orthodox Church was on the radar of the relevant MPs.

The application was eventually assessed and scored highly enough to secure funding for both projects. This was the first time that the Macedonian Orthodox Community of NSW received any public funding, and they were grateful for my advice to secure it.

The CEO called me after the grant was approved. 'Thank you for helping the community,' he told me.

And I had – but I'd also helped myself.

Let me tell you about who regularly attends the Macedonian churches in Cabramatta and Roseberry: about 100 members of the Labor Party from Western Sydney electorates, that's who. The Macedonian-Australian community are natural Labor voters, and I had very visibly assisted their churches get much-needed grants.

My thinking had been: if these party members see me very actively helping out their church, they're going to be very happy with me and keep supporting me in the Labor Party, whether in local branch meetings or if I ever decided to run for an elected position. At the time, I was toying with the idea of running for Council. Being seen as a community hero in the influential Macedonian community would be the final feather in my cap if I decided to pull a preselection trigger – though the *Survivor* gods had other ideas. But at the time, I knew this would serve as an important achievement for my political résumé.

THE ENTIRE GOOD DEED HAD BEEN, FOR ME, AN EXERCISE IN PUBLICLY DEMONSTRATING MY WORTH TO THE COMMUNITY.

I used my knowledge of government processes for good. I showed my importance as a political enabler, as someone who can get things done. I'd manipulated a transparent, objective government grant process to help the local churches *and* for my personal reputational benefit. I had my communion wafer and ate it, too.

This may all sound slightly villainous, but remember this: the old Babushka who prays every Sunday at the Cabramatta church now has a ramp to make her visit safer. People in a wheelchair, like my friend Kiki Stojanoski, can now enter the inside of the Cabramatta church. And at the same time, the young Macedonian-Australian girls can use it as a runway for their TikToks while they wait for their parents and grandparents to finish worshipping inside during Easter. It was a win-win, but I kept *my* win quiet, leaving my church-helping altruism on full display.

THERE IS NOTHING WRONG WITH A CHARITABLE ACT THAT HELPS YOU, TOO. IF OPPORTUNITIES LIKE THESE PRESENT THEMSELVES, TAKE THEM; DON'T WORRY ABOUT WHETHER IT'S FOR THE 'RIGHT REASON'.

And if they don't, work out situations where you can manufacture them. What good deed now could pay off in the future? I'm not talking about anonymous donations or subtle assistance behind the scenes (though that might bless your soul more than your authority). These acts need to be public – declarations of your big, kind heart by doing a big, kind deed. You never know who is watching or what kind of benefit it may have.

So I knew exactly who to thank when I found my safety without power advantage on the very first day in the Australian outback. As I kissed the parchment and raised it to the cameras, I said for the first time what would soon become a King George catchphrase: 'Thank you, Macedonian Jesus!'

Of course I meant it – old MJ was probably shining down on me because I helped out those crumbling old churches. But I also threw the line in specifically for all those members of the church who might be watching. The name Macedonia was being used in a positive way on national television, and I am definitely proud of my Macedonian ancestry. All from one good deed. Praise be to Macedonian Jesus.

THERE IS NOTHING BETTER THAN A WELL-PLACED THREAT

'If you don't back me on this, I will *never* speak to you again.'

It's quite the threat – especially when it's delivered to your own father.

We were standing in a boarding queue at Sydney airport, about to get on a flight to New Zealand. It was a rare 'boys holiday': me, Dad and my twin brother Steve, flying off to Wellington together to watch the football team we all supported, the Western Sydney Wanderers, play an away game against Wellington Phoenix.

It was meant to be a special trip. Even though Steve and I were in our mid-twenties at the time, I had not gone away on a holiday with my dad and brother since we went on a road trip to the snow when Steve and I were in Year 7. And here I was, the moment before we hopped aboard, where I would sit elbow-to-elbow with my father for three and a half hours, threatening to cut all ties with him.

What could drive me to such an extreme moment?

Football club politics, of course.

A couple of years earlier, I'd joined the board of the Bankstown City Lions Football Club. The club is an institution in both the local Bankstown sporting society and broader Macedonian-Australian community in NSW. It is one of the great old ethnic clubs of Australian football.

My father and grandfather were foundational members in the 1980s, and my family always had a great connection to the club. But, as with all things related to the local Macedonian community, the club was riddled with internal factions, competing interests and opinions.

When you put 120 Macedonians together, there's always drama. Macedonians love nothing more than a snipe. The membership of the club was very political, divided into warring factions who would argue about how best to use limited resources and would hold board seats tightly to wield power. Picture *Succession*, except almost everyone is over 60,

Macedonian, and the issue at stake is whether or not we should buy a new set of goal posts.

I came to the club's board full of fresh ideas. I had always loved football, but I absolutely sucked at playing it. Better to make my mark off the field. I was a keen supporter of Bankstown City Lions and happened to be one of the few members who wasn't eligible for a pension.

But by the time I joined, the club was sadly in the start of a rapid decline. Just 10 years earlier, Bankstown City Lions were the two-times champion of NSW, pulling crowds of up to 7,000 people to watch their games. When the old National Soccer League folded in 2004, we were the strongest club in NSW, and could arguably claim to be the best club in Australia at the time.

Fast forward to 2012, the club had its first bad season in its history and had just been booted from the NSW Premier League to the Second Division. Just like in England, NSW has a football pyramid of three and sometimes four divisions, where clubs get promoted and relegated on an annual basis and slide between the different leagues. Bankstown's relegation to the Second Division was devastating to see, both as a fan and as a member of the club.

Bankstown had always overspent on players and was known as the club that splashed out whopper pay cheques. We used to have the finances to pay big money to big players, but without big crowds, I could see the writing on the wall.

But after the 2011 FIFA Women's World Cup, I could feel the local and global mindset shift towards fully embracing women's sport. I remember asking myself one night: 'Why doesn't Bankstown have a team in the NSW Women's League?' I could see that if the club didn't evolve from its glory days, we would soon be a thing of the past. I knew a women's team could help us take a big step into the future.

The ethnic clubs in Australian football were always the powerhouse clubs; they had the resources to succeed, thanks to public support and community fundraising. However, those same clubs usually ignored women's football. At the time in NSW, only Marconi Stallions (the Italians) and Sydney Olympic (the Greeks) had teams in the women's league. If those old ethnic clubs had women's teams, why didn't we?

So in mid-2012, I approached the club's board of directors after I saw that Football NSW had put out an expression of interest for two new clubs to join the Women's Third Division. The membership was rightfully angry that the club had just been relegated out of the NSW Premier League, and I could see that the money bag was going to dry up within 12 months. If the club didn't try to change very quickly, it would fold and die. I saw it as being beneficial to both myself and the club to help.

With the board's approval, I joined them on a temporary basis as a club director. This was a coup in and of itself, as seats on the board were so closely held. I turned all of my attention toward putting in an application to join the Women's Third Division. The other directors at the time were supportive, but they didn't think that Football NSW would grant the licence.

However, as you just learned, I have a particular knack for writing an application that ticks all the boxes. (I should start a side-hustle as a grant writer, really.) Surprisingly to everybody but me, our application was approved: the Bankstown City Lions were getting a women's team, and I was now a part of the club's board for at least 12 more months. Goals across the board, literally.

As a newly minted director, I took the opportunity to closely scrutinise the financial position of the club. Looking under the bonnet, I could see that things were even worse than I'd suspected. It was looking *dire*. The club's finances were solely reliant on game-day revenue and community sponsorship, and I anticipated that dropping out of the First Division would see that revenue fall by at least 80 per cent.

What the club needed was *stability*. We needed to stop that old-fashioned Macedonian sniping and war-mongering if we wanted to steady the ship and make sure we had a future. I was adamant that the new women's football program needed to succeed, as the club had a golden opportunity to become a leader in that space (which – spoiler alert – it is today).

But there were challenges. My godfather George Jackson, a respected businessman in the Macedonian and Bankstown community, was rallying to overhaul the club's board. It was all set to go down at the club's Annual General Meeting – always a full-on affair, with Macedonian men screaming and swearing at each other about every little item on the agenda.

I feared that it would mean more disunity at a time when we were bleeding cash, which could spell disaster for the club I had been trying to turn around. All this would happen while our rival football clubs continued to evolve, surely erasing our competitive advantage in South-West Sydney as a destination club.

I could see clearly who held influence over the club's membership: my godfather, my father and their friends. Men who had been around the club since its inception.

The members of the club listen to my dad, because the only people old Macedonian men listen to is other old Macedonian men. I thought this was exactly what was keeping the club stuck in the past, unable to see the opportunity something like a women's league presented.

I knew I needed my father's help to maintain control, but as the AGM approached − with our trip to Wellington coming right before it − he appeared unwilling to bat for me, clearly uncomfortable with having to choose between his son and his friend, my godfather.

'What do you want me to do?' he'd say, and shrug. I told him in no uncertain terms that he needed to call George Jackson's supporters and tell them to stand down, stop the drama and let the current board secure a viable future for the club.

He ummed and aahed, and as we headed to the airport that morning, I knew I needed to take more extreme action.

There's great power in a well-placed threat, and it can be utilised to get your way. But there's a key ingredient upon which everything hinges, or the move can blow up in your face:

YOU HAVE TO MAKE YOUR THREAT FROM A POSITION OF POWER. YOU CAN'T THREATEN FROM THE BOTTOM; YOU ALREADY NEED TO HAVE SOME LEVERAGE. YOU NEED TO BE CERTAIN YOUR THREAT WILL BE HEARD, AND TAKEN SERIOUSLY.

Let's take one of the easiest threats you can exploit in the workplace: announcing that you're looking for another job. Maybe you've been getting nowhere in climbing the career ladder. Perhaps you're feeling overworked and underappreciated, and requests to lighten your load have been ignored. You want to leave – but it would also be better (and easier) to stay, if the circumstances were more in your favour.

This can be a great time to dangle a small threat and see where it gets you. Threats don't have to be delivered in a threatening way, though; you don't have to storm into a conference room, beating your chest and bellowing that you're going to quit.

THREATS DON'T HAVE TO BE DELIVERED IN A THREATENING WAY.

Instead, you can simply, softly, quietly mention that you've started to cast your eye around for other employment opportunities, either casually in the tearoom or more formally in a meeting. (You don't *actually* need to be looking; whether it's the truth or a lie, the effect is the same.)

The aim is to get your boss to wake up to your dissatisfaction, and realise they'd better figure out a way to keep you. You also have to be prepared for the possibility you might have to follow through on your threat, if need be – only throw your chips on the table if you're ready to lose. But all going to plan, you shouldn't have to.

But before you do this, take stock of your situation – and the wider state of the marketplace. Ask yourself these questions, and be honest with yourself:

- Are you a high performer, going above and beyond at work in a demonstrable way?
- Are you undervalued, and could get more money in a similar role elsewhere?
- Would it be difficult and time-consuming to replace you if you left?
- Are you contributing to the success of the business?

If you answered yes to most or all of these positions, then you can threaten from a position of power. Any good boss should hear alarm bells if an employee of your status is looking to find greener pastures.

But if you take long lunches, leave at 5pm on the dot and phone it in on Fridays – or if you're a hard-working employee in a market where there is a queue of capable candidates eager to take your job – then a threat can blow up in your face.

'Boss, I want you to know I'm unhappy here and am starting to think about other employment opportunities.'

'Ah, that's a shame. Can you clear out your desk by lunch?'

That's not how you want that meeting to go. You may have to bide your time until your circumstances change and you'll be in a position of power that enables you to utilise such threats as tools. Or if you don't want to wait that long, lead with the carrot rather than the stick: Compile evidence of your good performance at work, and you can start presenting a case for a reward.

Threats can also be a powerful tool to get things done in your community. You can do this collectively by manoeuvring the levers of politics. So many of us feel completely disengaged from the political process. Have you ever contacted your local Member of Parliament? It's likely

99 per cent of the population haven't – and that's just the way some lazy politicians, who'd rather their constituents left them alone, like it.

But let me let you in on a little secret from inside politics: there's nothing that scares a member more than a group of voters who've banded together with a threat to use their voting power to get what they want.

Say you and your neighbours are frustrated with a road safety issue on your street. You're in a residential area, but drivers constantly ignore the speed limit and hoon down the road. It's noisy and it's dangerous – kids play out there. A simple speed hump would solve the issue overnight.

Here's how you get things done: a letter signed by all the residents of the street, sent to your local member, declaring that they will not have your vote in the next election until something is done to make the street safer.

To a politician, a letter like that is about as scary to read as coming home to 'I KNOW WHAT YOU DID LAST SUMMER' scrawled in blood on your mirror.

Again, you're operating from a position of power: politicians live and die by their voters, and every single vote counts. Lose a whole street? Well, that's just something they can't afford.

YOU MIGHT NOT HAVE POWER TO THREATEN SOLO, BUT YOU DO AS A GROUP.

Or sometimes, an individual holds enough power alone. Which brings me back to my father.

'If you don't back me on this, I will *never* speak to you again,' I told him.

There was tension in the air as we shuffled forward to board our flight, tickets in hand. I could see the people in line in front of us turning around, no doubt hoping they were sat nowhere near this unfolding family feud once they got on board.

I looked over at my father. He seemed stunned at the threat I'd just made. As the implications of my threat fully registered, he was speechless. My brother Steve was mute as ever, staring intently at his phone and pretending he couldn't hear the bomb I'd just dropped.

Nothing is more important to my father than family; the thought of one of his boys cutting him out of his life? Unthinkable.

The thought of his son disowning him, playing out in front of an audience of 120 gossipy old Macedonian men? He'd never live it down.

Would I have stopped talking to my father forever if he hadn't followed my wishes? Of course not. Eventually I'd have thawed (although the holiday would've been very frosty). But I had hit him where it hurt, letting him know in an instant just how serious I was about this issue. And I *was* serious; the threat would have been empty without it.

My father agreed there and then to back me instead of my godfather, and Air New Zealand flight 248 to Wellington departed on time and with a big family rift narrowly avoided. Sadly for me I was seated next to my dad in economy class and had absolutely no elbow room for three and a half hours, but at least the discomfort was physical, not emotional.

By the time we'd arrived at our hotel, he was working the phones, calling the other members and sending the message that this was a time for board stability. They received the memo loud and clear, which meant I could continue to pursue my vision for the club.

Honestly, I think the scariest part of my threat for Dad was the prospect of having to rely solely on my brother for conversation during our holiday. *That* would be quite the punishment.

CHAPTER 11

KEEP YOUR CLOSET FREE OF SKELETONS

In general, when battling with my enemies, I like to turn to the sword rather than the shield. You always have a greater degree of control and influence over people if your strategy is offence rather than defence.

However, being on the offensive also tends to invite more heat. You must always be aware that your opposition in any situation, whether it is a rival in the workplace or a cousin at a family gathering, may be willing to use your secrets against you. In these cases, the best way to disarm them is actually to disarm yourself: to give up your secrets so that they can't be used to hurt you.

WHEN BATTLING WITH MY
ENEMIES, I LIKE TO TURN
TO THE SWORD RATHER
THAN THE SHIELD. YOU
ALWAYS HAVE A GREATER
DEGREE OF CONTROL AND
INFLUENCE OVER PEOPLE
IF YOUR STRATEGY IS
OFFENCE RATHER
THAN DEFENCE.

Everyone has their closet full of skeletons — and anyone who wants to ruin you would do anything to get a peek inside.

BUT INSTEAD OF KEEPING THE DOOR LOCKED, THE BEST WAY TO DEAL WITH THE SKELETONS IN YOUR CLOSET IS TO SWEEP THEM OUT YOURSELF.

This is a valuable life lesson that I learned through personal experience, coming to terms with my own sexuality.

It took me until my mid-twenties to both internally accept and publicly acknowledge that I was a gay man. People from different communities and backgrounds go through their own journey of acceptance and discovery, and I am a product of my community. I know I present as a very confident person now, but this wasn't necessarily the case when as a teenager in high school, when I felt like if I accepted my sexuality, it would be a burden to my family.

I don't have many regrets in life, but wasting my teenage years and early twenties pretending to be interested in women when I knew deep down that I wasn't is probably my only one.

I even genuinely attempted to try having a relationship with a woman, convincing myself that it would be the best course of action for my future. Ah, the good old 'beard' strategy: a word people use for a partner that provides the other with a misconceived notion of 'stability' and 'nuclear family values' – two things I never truly wanted or needed.

You live and learn through life, and eventually I made the call that I needed to make: that I have one life to live and I am going to sure as hell live my best one.

Accepting my own sexuality as a gay man was the final push I needed to reach the level of confidence I now exude every day. Having my skeleton come out of the closet was not an easy step for me, but once I let him out, it was liberating. And one of the surprising by-products?

NOW THAT MY SECRET WAS NO LONGER A SECRET, MY ENEMIES HAD LESS COLLATERAL TO USE AGAINST ME.

By freeing myself from my own falsified narrative, I took my control of the story back.

What working in politics taught me more than anything else is that your opposition is often willing to use any aspect of your personal life to damage your reputation. For me, this was who I chose to date. Being from Bankstown, being gay and being political guaranteed one thing: somebody was going to try to use the fact that I am gay in order to defame my name in my community and to coerce my behaviour and actions. Whispers are one of the most dangerous wrecking balls that can destroy your reputation; gossip can be more damaging than the truth. Luckily for me, by the time they started swirling, I had already come out. But this didn't stop people from trying.

And if there's one thing that the Macedonian community loves, it is gossip! I clearly remember two women coming up to me at one football club meeting to breathlessly report some hearsay: 'George, somebody in the community saw you kissing a man behind the grandstand at Jensen Park!'

This was news to me, because I don't think I had ever kissed a man at a Bankstown game at Jensen Park. But I knew these two women, friends on paper, were passive aggressively threatening me with a fishing exercise about my sexuality. This is how Macedonian women make friends and manipulate you – by using any secret or gossip they can against you. (I've learned from the best.)

From a political perspective, somebody in the Labor Party had seen me at a gay bar in Oxford Street – Sydney's gay district, for the uninitiated. I remember one time being specifically threatened with the words: 'We are going to tell everybody who knows you that you're gay.' I told them they were a few years too late for that to be much of a bombshell to anyone. I had been going out on dates in Bankstown with men for a while by that stage, yet if somebody in the community saw me kissing a man – *escandalo*! Any sting in their comments or barbs in their threats would instantly be diffused, though, as I would shrug it off. Gossip stops being dangerous when it becomes fact.

As you've surely noticed, I love my hometown of Bankstown almost more than anything (except my dog, Douglas). However, I have to admit that it has a more complicated view on members of the LGBTQIA+ community, with attitudes slowly changing more favourably with time.

I've never had a problem being an out gay man in Bankstown. Aside from high school, where teenagers made gay jokes at just about everybody, I have never even experienced or seen homophobia on the streets of Bankstown. Do I parade down Saigon Bankstown City Plaza with a rainbow flag? No. Have I been on coffee dates with men in Bankstown? Yes!

I'm not preachy about my sexuality; it's a part of me, but not all of me. In fact, I wouldn't even be addressing it in this book if it wasn't for one simple reason: that a secret loses its power as soon as it is spoken. From my perspective, once I had discharged the skeleton out of my closet, I became impervious to any ability that such a secret would have to damage me. It took a long time for me to learn a valuable lesson:

IF YOU DON'T HAVE ANY SECRETS, YOU DON'T HAVE ANY FEAR.

By the time it came to film my first television experience, I had made the conscious decision that I would publicly and visibly acknowledge my sexuality. I was 31 by then, and though I had been out as a gay man for many years, on paper, I was 'straight acting'. I guess I've always been a bit of a mixed bag: I love football and poker and I'm from Western Sydney, but at the same time I'm obsessed with Eurovision, hardly a bastion of heterosexuality.

At camp in the Outback for my first *Survivor* season, I therefore was very open with my castmates about my dating life while the cameras rolled. I was out and proud with them, not hiding myself one bit. What I was almost certain would make the edit was an on-camera joke that I made with a producer during a confessional. She was interviewing me after tribe swap, which had worked in my favour: I'd spent the last two weeks playing in a minority alliance where I never had the numbers to control the tribe, and now it looked like I was about to wrest back some power.

Producer: George, what does it feel like to be on top?

Me: Oh my god, I'm a top now! I'll have to update my Grindr settings.

(Don't get it? Google it. Maybe not while you're at work.)

But watching the season back, no mention of my sexuality ever made the final cut. And that wasn't because they didn't have time to build the storyline. On my first season of *Australian Survivor*, I broke a worldwide *Survivor* record for screentime. I had about 22 per cent of the total screentime over 24 episodes and 159 individual interview confessionals that made the final edit. The second placed holder for airtime is *also* me, with 156 confessionals after my Heroes v Villains season in Samoa. There must have been countless hours of footage of my conversations about failed dates and relationships and hook-ups taken over the 24/7 filming period. And not once did they ever include anything that mentioned my sexuality.

In some ways, I liked the fact that the editing team did not feel the need to raise who I date as a point of interest about me. This was a sign of progress in many ways: a casual acceptance that I didn't need to be tokenised to be interesting. The audience was not fascinated by me because I was gay – they were fascinated by my personality, political skills, Bankstown street smarts and ability to entertain.

However, post-production keeping my sexuality under wraps (intentionally or otherwise) made for some awkward moments when the season aired. Hayley Leake, my dear friend who was awarded the title of Sole Survivor instead of me by a bitter jury, would talk multiple times a day with me while our first season was airing. We would regularly help each other navigate this new experience of having millions of Australians and people around the world watching us on TV each night. She told me what her friends were saying about me as they watched. *We're convinced George is gay*, they'd tell her with a giggle. *George is gay, and he doesn't know it.*

I'm no clueless closet case. Yes, I am gay – and yes, I do know it! Hayley would laugh and tell them the same thing. I would bemoan this intel, thinking: *Maybe this is why I am still single!*

While I didn't particularly care that Australia didn't know my preference for men after my first *Survivor* experience, the second time around, I wanted to be a bit more proactive. I wore pride socks into the Samoan jungle, and later on in the game, I wore Shonee's bikini to cheer up my friend Liz (after I had voted out her best friend Shonee).

In the end, my actual TV 'outing' came about in a funny, rapid-fire moment that apparently many viewers didn't expect. By that time I'd formed what we called the Spice Girls alliance with Shonee and Liz, so I figured that everyone should have probably picked up that I was batting for the other team. We were loving our new alliance, but it was under threat, and Shonee had become convinced that if any 'big player' like me went home, that she would be targeted immediately to be voted off.

Pulling me aside at camp, cameras trained on us, she announced: 'I've already lost two girls … I can't lose the only gay. That would be a crime against humanity.'

It was the first reference about my sexuality to make the television edit, and I'm glad Australia got to see a bit more of that side of me on my second season.

I know for some fans watching at home who'd never twigged, it was a bit of a spit-take moment, but for me, it was a win for casual queer representation. (And less of a win for Shonee, whom I voted out soon after anyway.)

The media was less subtle and tried to make my story their own. I appeared on *The Kyle and Jackie O Show* during my post-*Survivor* media blitz, and I thought the interview went well. Like any good Western Sydney boy, I'm a fan of Kyle and Jackie O, and they were their usual fun and exuberant selves. At one point they asked me to clarify Shonee's comment from the show and asked if she had outed me. I told them she didn't, and that I'd been out for years.

But shortly after the interview had finished, a post went out on the show's socials announcing that King George from *Survivor* had just 'come out' on their show. I was livid. Please! If I was going to come out publicly via the media like that, do you think I'd do it on a radio show?

Imagine if I hadn't made that fateful decision to follow my happiness back in my mid-20s. I'd be miserable. I'd be making other people miserable. And there'd definitely be no King George on *Survivor* – no way would I have put myself under the reality-TV microscope with so much to hide. Instead, I'd have probably been watching it at home with a wife, trying to hide my wide-eyed reaction every time the camera lingered on a buff male player's tanned abs.

No thank you.

TOO MANY OF US LIVE LIKE THAT – NOT FOLLOWING WHAT WE REALLY WANT, SETTLING FOR A LIFE OF STAYING HOME WATCHING TV, INSTEAD OF BEING ON IT. LIFE IS FOR LIVING, SO GO OUT AND GRAB IT.

So wear what your enemies say about you with pride: too gay, too ethnic, too fat, too nerdy – take those arrows people might throw your way and turn them into your armour. The best defensive tool that you could have in life is to be true to yourself and to own it. You control the power in this situation, and you can remove any ammunition that your enemies could use against you.

WEAR WHAT YOUR ENEMIES SAY ABOUT YOU WITH PRIDE.

MANIPULATE A BAD BOSS – AND BE A GOOD ONE

I've had my fair share of good and bad bosses. I've dealt with micro-managers who want to check my work before I've even had a chance to finish it, 'always on' bosses who wonder why I'm not responding to an email at 5pm on a Sunday, and bosses who were just plain rude, not even acknowledging my existence unless it's to bark orders. I particularly remember a boss at an early, I-don't-get-paid-enough-to-put-up-with-this job who used to time my breaks down to the second: 'George – you were 40 seconds over on your lunch break. Don't let it happen again.' (It may or may not have been when I worked at the Kmart Bankstown checkout.)

Some bad bosses – like that clock-watcher – just have to be endured until you get a better job. But a lot of crappy bosses can be dealt with in subtle ways to make life easier for yourself.

I had one particularly frustrating boss when I was working in government who made my job more difficult from the day she arrived. She'd just been promoted into the role and it seemed to me that she wanted to prove that she was up for the job, but her way of doing so was by blocking the workflow, holding things up so she could demonstrate how committed she was to her new role.

Time and again, myself and the other members of our small team would submit briefs and letters for her to review, only to have her knock them back, insisting they weren't good enough and demanding changes. My output had been more than fine for my previous manager – why was everything suddenly an issue? I knew this new manager wanted to demonstrate that she was taking her job seriously.

'That brief?' I could imagine her saying to our director. 'It's coming – I've had to crack the whip to get it absolutely perfect.'

There were a couple of problems with this situation: not only was it slowing down my work processes, making me re-work standard documents I could do once with my eyes closed, but it was also threatening to impact my reputation. Suddenly, I was in danger of becoming known as the guy who couldn't get simple tasks right the first, second or even third time.

How did I deal with this sudden work happiness nosedive? Simple. I tackled the problem at its root. Too many people don't do this, focusing their resentments at the surface-level issue rather than taking a wider look at the situation at hand, and why it's got so *out* of hand. I know it sounds counterintuitive,

BUT RATHER THAN FOCUSING ON MAKING *YOUR* LIFE EASIER, SOMETIMES YOU SHOULD MAKE YOUR PROBLEM PERSON'S LIFE EASIER INSTEAD.

This is what I decided to do with my never-satisfied manager. First, I identified her goal. I did this by asking myself some questions. What did she want out of her new job? In this case, it was to look competent and capable as a manager to her superior. Why did she want to do that? Because she wanted to keep climbing up that public sector chain. And what was the result? That meant riding me and the rest of her new team so she could cultivate a reputation as a tough taskmaster.

Of course, I had a different motivation: I was a mid-tier bureaucrat in a government department. I just wanted to get my work done and go home on time. How could I help her achieve what she wanted, while still benefiting me? If I could make her happier at work, maybe she'd stop making me so miserable.

I knew I needed to go around her to sort my situation out; there was no way she'd listen to me directly. I also knew I needed to do this as stealthily as possible. That's the thing about ruling from the backseat: if you do it well, the person in the driver's seat doesn't realise you're actually the one driving. If they do, they are gonna yank on that parking brake as forcefully as they possibly can. You'll be kaput.

An opportunity presented itself when I had a meeting with my director, who was one rung higher than my new boss in the government ladder. It was one of those semi-regular 'catch-up' evaluations that bureaucrats are so fond of. (Wonder why nothing gets done in government? Everyone's stuck in a meeting.)

I knew I had to tread carefully. There was nothing to be gained in openly complaining about my manager; 'she

THAT'S THE THING ABOUT RULING FROM THE BACKSEAT: IF YOU DO IT WELL, THE PERSON IN THE DRIVER'S SEAT DOESN'T REALISE YOU'RE ACTUALLY THE ONE DRIVING.

makes me pay too much attention to my work' is not exactly a grievance that'll be taken seriously. Any attempts to grumble about this new regime could just paint me as a bludger.

So I started by praising my new manager. I'd already identified that looking good in front of her superiors was her main goal in all this, so I made sure they knew she was doing a good job.

Then I approached the problem from the side. I asked how my director was finding the work rate from our little section of the department lately. After considering it for a second, my boss's boss said that she'd noticed that fewer things had been landing on her desk recently.

This is lesson number two:

ALWAYS SEE IF YOU CAN GET YOUR BOSS TO SPOT A PROBLEM WITHOUT YOU HAVING TO POINT IT OUT.

Give them all the information and let them come to their own conclusions. This is the one time where you *don't* want credit for your work. If you can make them believe that this was their own brilliant realisation, then they will carry the torch forward without you risking being burned.

It gave me the chance to spitball potential reasons for the reduced workflow with her; I was now acting as her Watson-like assistant, helping her solve a crime (that I secretly knew was being committed by the newly minted middle manager). I mentioned that we were finding our work needed a lot more revisions in recent months. I noted that letters and briefs I used to be able to send out quite quickly now returned to my desk several times to be revised, so I wasn't able to produce as much work.

I said all this free of any discernible emotion or bias. I hadn't even mentioned my manager's name. I was just stating the bald facts of my current working situation, without recrimination.

I let the director come to their own conclusions about what was happening – and she did. Soon after that meeting, it became apparent that my manager had been taken aside and told to pick up the pace with her communications. Briefs and letters very soon stopped coming back to me two or three times with pointless revisions.

And because of how I'd approached the situation – no complaint, no blame, just a casual chat with her superior, in which I was also careful to praise her – there was no blowback for me. My manager was none the wiser that I'd orchestrated this improvement in my situation. This was a case of identifying the two competing priorities of my manager in her new role (to seem competent) with that of our director (to move the workload through quickly). In the catch up between my manager and director, my director would've noted that the team is happy with the new manager, but it was my director's priority to increase the pace of delivery of the work.

Manipulating situations – and bad bosses – in the workplace is all about checking your emotions at the door and choosing carefully how you're going to present your information.

YOU HAVE TO IDENTIFY THE POWER STRUCTURES IN PLACE, KNOW WHERE YOU SIT WITHIN THEM AND PICK YOUR BATTLES ACCORDINGLY.

To do that, you need to know who to approach for your specific problem. As a rule, look to those one or two rungs ahead of your boss instead of going straight to the top: they're the ones who'll most be able – and willing – to affect a change in your situation. Other times it's a case of identifying which person in power might have the most sympathetic ear to your problem, and working on your relationship with them. To work this out, that's where networking comes in to play. Don't be the person who always skips after-work drinks on a Friday; it's a great opportunity to speak to people when their guards are down and get a sense of where everyone's loyalties lie.

What about if you *are* the boss? Let me give you a couple of simple tips on how to rule well. These suggestions not only will help you become a benevolent sovereign, but will also benefit over-stressed, underpaid workers everywhere.

Firstly, you must assemble a team you can trust and rely on. A king can reign forever, so long as they have their loyal subjects on side. That's really the key to being a good boss – keeping the support of those underneath you. This can take some time, but a king is nothing without his subjects. You need a team of people who are good at their specific jobs so that you can focus on yours. But as a people leader, if you build a loyal and engaged team who believe that your decisions are the correct ones, then it will make your life and workflow a lot easier.

A KING CAN REIGN FOREVER, SO LONG AS THEY HAVE THEIR LOYAL SUBJECTS ON SIDE.

DON'T BE AFRAID OF TALENT: BUILD A STRONG SQUAD, TRUST THEM TO DO THEIR JOBS AND IT'S LESS WORK FOR YOU IN THE LONG RUN.

Secondly, you have to be confident in your decision-making. Nobody respects a king (or queen) who can't make a damn decision. You don't need to rush the process – and a good leader will always consult for expert advice – but making tough calls is so much of what being a leader is. Explain the reasoning for your decision to take your subjects on the journey with you – never just rule from the balcony and then go back inside once you've given your orders. Then stand firm in your decisions and you'll earn respect and support.

Lastly – and this is perhaps the most important point – treat your subjects with fairness and respect. This is key when it comes to retaining good quality people: the number one reason people change jobs is because they feel unappreciated where they are. Thank and reward your team for good performance – it can be anything from a pay rise to a shout-out in a weekly email.

If you follow these commandments, you'll have amassed a legion of loyal subjects – and through kindness, not fear. Ruling with an iron fist won't work if there is nobody to rule, as your staff will have all moved to greener pastures.

Each and every person experiences office politics. It is basic human nature. But if you can identify what each person in the chain of command needs, you will be on the front foot to being able to manipulate your work life to suit you for the better.

CHAPTER 13

USE STEREOTYPES TO YOUR ADVANTAGE

Stereotyping people can get a bad rap – and with good reason. I'm from a non-English-speaking background in Sydney's western suburbs, so I know a thing or two about being negatively stereotyped. People's immutable elements – their age, gender, sexuality and ethnicity – should not be used against them to deny them of opportunity. However, on the poker table, and in certain other situations, using stereotypes to your advantage can give you an upper hand.

I quickly learned a big lesson when my poker game moved out of the shag-pile carpet and dark timber tables of the upstairs living room in my parents' house. No longer was I playing with my schoolmates, who were all in the same position as me, scraping together the $50 buy-in from their parents or after-school jobs. Now, I was faced with a broader cross-section of players, and I had to get a read on my opponents very quickly if I wanted to succeed.

I pay close attention to my fellow poker players when I first meet them, making quick, calculated guesses about who I'm up against. Clothes are an easy one. Is a player well-dressed, sporting designer labels or wearing a nice watch? You can make a few safe assumptions from this: they have money, they're not as afraid to lose their cash as other players, and they might feel more comfortable playing aggressively.

Contrast that with, say, a modestly dressed older Italian lady (I've played against more than a few in Western Sydney). Someone like this is probably paying with retirement money, meaning she's most likely going to be a more conservative player, wary of putting herself in any position that could lose her too much cash. Less risk, less reward. They see an ace, get excited, and bet.

In poker though, like life, it always pays to test these assumptions. There's always the possibility your opponent's *only* designer outfit is the one they're wearing; that it's all for show, to project a certain image at the poker table. Maybe that pensioner invested wisely over the years and has millions to blow at the table.

That's where the social charm offensive comes in. As I've mentioned, I'm not a stone-faced gargoyle at the game table – or off it. I make conversation with my opponents to try to glean as much additional information about them as possible. Who is this person? Where do they live? What do they do for work? Get as much free material as possible before you make a tactical decision about how you're going to play against them.

If I think I've made the correct call about a player, I can either bluff them or play hard against them. That's when a little bit of poker luck needs to come into play:

YOU HAVE TO BET ON YOURSELF, THAT YOUR INSTINCT AND JUDGEMENT CALL ON A PERSON IS RIGHT.

Of course, I'm sure clever poker players used stereotyping to get one up on *me* when I first started playing at clubs and tournaments, too. I was young, a uni student just looking to make money to spend on the weekend. I tried my best to project an air of confidence but I have no doubt my youth gave me away; I had more bravado than I had experience back then, and had to grow into my poker game.

Every time I play on the poker circuit now, I get automatically stereotyped as 'that guy from TV' or 'the *Survivor* villain'. If I am at more of a pub or club-style game against a social player, they are more likely to gamble against me to tell their friends and family that they beat King George in a hand. Because I know this is how they are pigeon-holing me, I can use my *own* stereotype to my advantage and play in a way they're not expecting.

STEREOTYPING IS A TWO-WAY STREET: PEOPLE ARE SIZING YOU UP, TOO. AND AS LONG AS YOU'RE AWARE OF THIS, YOU CAN MESS WITH THEM.

If you project a certain aura, people might make the wrong assumption about you. This allows you to play in an unexpected way that confuses them and makes winning harder.

People often wonder why I seemed to be one step ahead of the play each and every time on *Survivor*. The answer is simple: I always made assumptions on what I thought people would do in certain situations, and I factored that into how I would play my hand at the individual point in time. I stereotyped them to guess the most likely thing they would do, and I was nearly always right. When I met people for the first time, I gathered information so I could make a judgement call about their character, subtly tested my assumptions and continually adjusted them as I got to know them better. First impressions count, but they're not always correct – especially if you meet people in circumstances where they're putting on a show, be it at a poker table, in the boardroom or in front of a prime-time camera crew.

There have been about 70 seasons of *Survivor* globally, split across the US, UK, Australia and South Africa. More often than not, the same kind of person gets voted out early: smaller/weaker players, older players, or a vote based on gender lines. I was very aware of these assumptions when I played *Survivor* the first time. As was normal, my Brains tribe was internally split between the 'weak' and the 'strong'. It was very frustrating, and clichéd, but it was also bad for my longer-term prospects if we went on a losing run. Even though I was not under immediate risk of having my torch snuffed, over the medium term, my prospects did not look good if the Brains tribe kept voting off the 'weak' players. This is how I was stereotyped by others.

When I got back to camp on Night Two after playing my Safety Without Player advantage, I was the only person with the courage to address the elephant in the room: half the tribe made assumptions on Rachel, Cara and Baden based on their age, and Wai and I because of our perceived lack of strength. When I was asked why I saved everyone, I said: 'Because people think you're old,' pointing to Rachel, 'and you're weak,' pointing to Wai. Everybody thought it, the people watching at home knew it, but I brought the sledgehammer home in the middle of the night. If I didn't, those stereotypes would have stuck, the game would have been boring and I would've been cast aside very early in the Outback after Wai, Rachel and Cara had been voted out.

I knew the stereotype of each player, and even more, that they wouldn't like that assumption about them. By bringing it to the fore, I set in train a motion of events that would stop those stereotypes from being factors in voting people off.

IF YOU CAN TAKE THE STING OUT OF THE INSULT, IT LOSES ITS POWER.

Stereotypes can be good and bad. What you always need is an open mind with a calculated guess based on the information at hand to set the parameters to control the unknown. If you test assumptions and take the reigns of the situation by keeping on the front foot, you can manipulate stereotypes to work for you rather than against you.

GATHER INFORMATION BEFORE YOU EVEN NEED IT

When it comes to manipulating your way around a situation, information is power. The more you know about your opponent, the better placed you'll be to get one over on them.

It's a skill I honed when I was a campaign director for the 2015 Bankstown Labor state election campaign. My duties spread into just about every element of organising the campaign – including some good old-fashioned dirt-digging.

The moment our opposition announced who was running against us, I instantly hopped online for a social-media stalk. I'd go through Facebook profiles, saving every public photo I could get my hands on. I'd do detailed Google searches,

WHEN IT COMES TO
MANIPULATING YOUR WAY
AROUND A SITUATION,
INFORMATION IS POWER.
THE MORE YOU KNOW
ABOUT YOUR OPPONENT,
THE BETTER PLACED YOU'LL
BE TO GET ONE OVER
ON THEM.

looking for information on their past business dealings and media appearances – anything I could get. I'd take screenshots of web profiles and articles and save the screenshot with the date visible.

TO BEAT YOUR ENEMY, YOU HAVE TO UNDERSTAND HOW THEY THINK. IF YOU SEARCH THROUGH THEIR HISTORY, YOU CAN LEARN THEIR STRENGTHS AND, HOPEFULLY, THEIR WEAKNESSES.

The first step is observing them. I'm not suggesting you go all private investigator, ruffling through their rubbish and stalking them in a nondescript rented Hyundai. Not only is that definitely illegal, it's also a waste of time. The internet is now public life's front porch, and you should use it to your advantage to get into the mind of your enemies.

That can mean gathering information before you're even sure of what it is you're looking for.

Which is exactly what I did. In the three months leading up to the election, every time the Liberal candidate in question posted a photo of himself on social media, I would save it. Every time he'd post a photo at a Liberal party event, I'd drag and drop it into my desktop 'dirt file'. I didn't have a plan yet as to what I'd do with all of these images. I just knew that the more information I had, the better.

Good for us, he didn't win the election that year – Tania Mihailuk worked close to 24/7 as an MP, and a good campaign got a positive result despite a cashed-up Liberal and Independent running against her. The 'dirt file' remained untouched on my computer. I never needed it in the end during the campaign period.

But Bankstown is like a big village where people's paths always cross. A few months after the 2015 election, I was sitting in a Labor branch meeting when in walked a new 'member' of the party. He'd just signed up and wanted to join Condell Park Branch. To me, his face looked familiar. I am not the best at remembering names, but I can remember faces from years back. I turned to my Labor boss and whispered: 'I know that man.'

At first I wasn't sure where I knew him from, but then it hit me: he'd made a fair few appearances on my campaign 'dirt file'.

I went home that night and checked the photos. I had picture after picture of the unsuccessful Liberal candidate, the person at the centre of my search – but his volunteers were in a lot of them, too. And there he was, in photo after photo: this person off the street supposedly wanting to join the Labor party, who just a few months prior was enthusiastically campaigning for the Liberals. I even had pictures of him in Liberal T-shirts saved on file. Busted.

I could guess what his sudden defection to Labor actually was: an attempt to take control of the numbers of the Condell Park Branch. Why would this Liberal campaigner have any interest in Labor or helping to elect Labor candidates? More likely he'd been instructed to join Condell Park Branch to destabilise the control of the legitimate party members who were running it. These included a 90-year-old former neighbour of Paul Keating and a 102-year-old World War II veteran. I wanted to make sure their voices were heard, not his.

Hard work always pays off, particularly in a heated environment like the inner machinations of a political party. Because I had the evidence, I knew I had this fake member snookered. I could immediately make the first attack before he'd even know I'd clued on to his nefarious move. While a group of organised people banding together – forming an alliance, to use a *Survivor* term – to overthrow a committee isn't against party rules, doing it with fake members is.

My action was swift. Armed with my evidence, I coordinated a charge to the mysterious Labor Internal Appeals Tribunal to have this person expelled from the party and their membership application rejected. To join a party and be a political member, you usually have to agree with the principles of that party. One simple Labor rule for membership eligibility is an obvious one – not to have campaigned against Labor in an election. This person that had the charges placed against them was present and seated a few metres across from me, and at first feigned ignorance to the accusation of having actively campaigned for the Liberal candidate for Bankstown at the recent election. But it's pretty hard to defend your position when presented with photos of yourself smiling with the Liberal party candidate at a party event, wearing their T-shirt, and handing out their flier.

Eventually, this man's membership was rejected. Who knows what would have happened if I hadn't spotted him, his smiling face stored in the deep recesses of my mind.

So don't be afraid to get your hands a little dirty; dirt that I had dug about political rivals ended turning to gold at a later date. This is the power of collating information on the people you need to keep in check: you never know when it'll come in handy.

CHAPTER 15

WATCH HOW YOUR ENEMIES CELEBRATE THEIR WINS

There's one profession that always makes me chuckle whenever I see them quoted in tabloids like the *Daily Mail*: 'body language expert.'

'Body language expert reveals what our PM and the US President think of each other.'

'Prince Harry subtly snubbed King Charles at the coronation, body language expert claims.'

'Body language experts share the five signs your partner is cheating on you.'

I don't know who these experts are – they're rarely quoted by name – but frankly, I'm offended none of these newspapers have ever called me to give them some insight. I may not have some bogus online degree in human behaviour, but I do have something much more helpful: a decade of experience at the poker table, working in politics and living in Bankstown.

I'm constantly amazed by just how bad most people are at reading one of the most obvious bits of information available to all of us in any social situation. Body language can tell us all so much, and for those who take the time to pick up the signals, it can give you all you need to softly guide a situation and get exactly what you want – all without your opponents even consciously realising what you're doing.

IF YOU'RE JUST PAYING ATTENTION TO WHAT PEOPLE ARE SAYING AND NOT WHAT THEIR BODY LANGUAGE IS INDICATING, YOU'RE MISSING THE MOST IMPORTANT PART OF THE STORY.

The key to becoming a body language expert of *Daily Mail* fame is to take the time to observe people – actually *observe* them. It's about letting go of thinking about yourself for a few minutes and focusing intently on someone else. No thinking

BODY LANGUAGE CAN TELL US ALL SO MUCH, AND FOR THOSE WHO TAKE THE TIME TO PICK UP THE SIGNALS, IT CAN GIVE YOU ALL YOU NEED TO SOFTLY GUIDE A SITUATION AND GET EXACTLY WHAT YOU WANT.

about how you look, instead training your eye on others and looking for those subtle – and sometimes, not-so-subtle – tells. My pilot friend Gerry Gelch from my second season of *Survivor* summed this up very simply: *mouths closed, eyes open.*

In a poker game, everyone at the table is trying desperately to conceal their own thoughts about the situation at hand. We all want our opponents to be in the dark about what cards we have and how we intend to play them. The problem is that on the whole, humans are nervous creatures who don't deal well under stress like that.

That's where common poker 'tells' come to the fore. A nervous player with a weak hand will avert their eyes, avoiding eye contact because they are less than comfortable about their situation. But don't just look at a player's eyes: keep your attention trained to their hands, particularly when they are handling their chips or cards. Shaking hands are one of the hardest bodily behaviours to mask. As many people who've done public speaking can attest, if you're nervous, or feeling under pressure, your hands will start rattling, and it's not something you can easily control.

I also like to look at how long it takes my opponents on the poker table to place bets. Those who tend to take their time to think through situations tend to overcook their hand.

They pause to consider their full range of options. Do I make a bet small enough so I can stay in the hand and win more money? Do I bet big, because I don't think I am ahead and need to force them out of the hand? Do I check (ie don't bet anything), to set a trap? There are lots of permutations, but the longer a round of betting takes, the more information and body language your opponents may give away. A fast player is generally someone who is confident: they know what they are doing, irrespective of the cards in play. This limits the opportunity to give something away in a tell through body language.

Of course, the subject of your attention may notice that you're zoning in on them closely. Don't worry about psyching them out − it is only to your benefit.

SENSING SCRUTINY, EVEN THE MOST PRACTISED SOCIAL PLAYER WILL START TO SQUIRM. THE LIARS WILL STAMMER, THE PEOPLE THAT CAN'T HANDLE THE SPOTLIGHT ON THEM WILL AVERT THEIR EYES.

Another great trick in any sort of confrontation, on or off the poker table, is to lean into the silences. This is particularly effective when you suspect the other person may be lying to you or withholding information. Let them linger. Drag them out to feel as awkward as a stripper at a funeral.

Even those with amazing willpower will usually find themselves rushing to fill the gap. But if you can hold strong, it nearly always means your conversation partner will jump in to fill it for you. That's when they can easily stumble and accidentally show their hand, giving up more information than they wanted.

Staying awkwardly silent doesn't come naturally to anyone; we are all hardwired to keep the ping pong ball of conversation bouncing smoothly back and forth. But being OK with feeling uncomfortable in silence will work to your benefit. Don't feel the need to rush to respond; count slowly to five or 10 after the other person has finished speaking, and watch them squirm as you stare them down, waiting for them to be the first to break the silence.

Poker is where I honed another important skill when it comes to body language: adjusting your *own* body language to hide your true intentions and make your opponents crumble.

A GREAT TRICK IN ANY SORT OF CONFRONTATION IS TO LEAN INTO THE SILENCES. PARTICULARLY WHEN YOU SUSPECT THE OTHER PERSON MAY BE LYING TO YOU OR WITHHOLDING INFORMATION. LET THEM LINGER.

First, you have to acknowledge your own tells, and actively work on them. Do your hands tremble when you're nervous? Keep them still, or under the table. Do you tend to rush through a bad hand? Slow it down, so your opponents are kept guessing.

HAVING AN AWARENESS OF YOUR OWN SIGNS OF WEAKNESSES IS THE ONLY WAY TO BE ABLE TO MASK THEM WHEN YOU NEED TO.

It's a delicate balance. You have to stay attuned to your fellow players, looking for signs of weakness, while also keeping your own guard up so as not to give anything away. These rules apply as much to meetings with your boss as they do high-stakes card hands.

Poker is all about putting maximum pressure on people. How do you do that? By acting like a winner. Cool, calm and collected – act like you've already won and are quietly counting your money in your head. A steady hand and a confident gaze has led me to victory during many a so-so poker game.

Do all that, and you don't need to have a winning hand. I often don't! The natural instinct for many people playing poker is to freeze up. Many people play conservatively because they're terrified of losing. If the other person thinks that you're stronger than them, usually they'll fold, or they won't call your bluff. It's a little like how I approached my *Survivor* auditions with a triple vodka's dose of artificial confidence, albeit in a less confrontational manner:

PROJECT AN AIR OF ASSURANCE, AND PEOPLE WILL BELIEVE IT.

Speaking of *Survivor* – a body language expert would have a field day on that show. I certainly did, picking up subtle hints along the way about where people's allegiances really lay, even when they were telling me the exact opposite.

In camp, most elements from the outside world are stripped away, so the simple things can really give away someone's true position. Who are they sleeping next to at night? Who do they serve the beans to first? Who do they rush to for comfort when they're upset, or who do they celebrate a win with? If it's not you, you're not in their alliance, no matter what they've been telling you in whispered encounters at the water well.

Of course, not every body language tell has to be subtle, as evidenced by one hilarious moment in my second season with Simon Mee, a real-life friend but fierce game rival of mine.

We'd already competed against each other in our first season, Brains v Brawn. He's an ex-bodybuilder, so you can guess which tribe he was on. We hadn't crossed paths once in almost a month in that first season, but Simon still blamed me for his blindside when he left the game with two hidden immunity idols in his pocket, the ultimate *Survivor* head-slap moment. What went to air credited the move to Hayley and Dani, but behind the scenes, Cara and I played an equally critical role in getting the ball in motion and turning all of his former Brawn allies against him. This set up an intense rivalry heading into Samoa for Heroes v Villains – and this time, we were both grouped into the 'Villains' tribe.

As some viewers loved to point out, we had a real Looney Tunes dynamic: I was the speedy roadrunner, always two steps ahead, while he was a big, buff Wile E Coyote, struggling to outsmart me – and always in danger of having an anvil dropped on his head.

As always happens in *Survivor* though, at certain points in the game you have to make nice with your enemies (or at least, pretend to). I made legitimate peace with Simon and wanted to work with him in the final stage of the game, but it appeared Simon's thirst for revenge stopped him from having the same intent. Simon did not pose a threat to my game with 12 players left: I wasn't banking on winning challenges like he was, so could have him as a number in my camp; Simon was at that point in the game disliked by a majority of the tribe, so he was always going to be targeted rather than me; and I thought that his predictable behaviour and tunnel vision would limit his opportunity to outmanoeuver me in the game. Despite these all seeming like negative things, it's actually a good combination for a *Survivor* ally: I'd rather keep some malleable human shields happy than have them wielded against me. So despite previous tension, I was willing to invite him to be part of my plans.

I reeled Simon in by giving him a lifeboat: a seat on my pirate ship in Samoa, where I was the Captain. From his perspective, it was his best shot for immediate survival, so he jumped on board. But Simon was not good at controlling his actions and body language in camp, which smelled like mutiny to me.

AT CERTAIN POINTS IN THE GAME YOU HAVE TO MAKE NICE WITH YOUR ENEMIES (OR AT LEAST, PRETEND TO).

I knew that Simon had become a so-called *Survivor* nerd in between filming in Cloncurry and Samoa. He was very cognisant of things like a correct voting record, and a desire to be both a swing vote (ie the deciding fourth vote in a 4-3-3 split) and voting for the correct target that ends up going home, rather than the back up. Making peace with Simon was a good game move, but at the same time, I needed to limit his powerbase so he would not have the ability or the capacity to jump off my ship.

Simon would talk a lot at camp. More often than not, it was with members of the minority alliance, like his old tribemates Shaun Hampson and Sam Webb. Simon had not had the chance to play the game with my now close allies Gerry Gelch and Matt Sharpe, but he always seemed more interested in boring (to me) life chats with the people who my alliance was trying to vote off.

Simon would also sleep alongside that minority alliance at night. Every night. For me, these were red flags that were being waved, indicating that Simon was still planning to vote me off at all costs, despite our recent peace treaty.

My suspicions were proven right once and for all at an immunity challenge with 10 players left in the game. It was a particularly tough one – we had to stack letters on a wobbly platform, eventually spelling out 'HEROES VS VILLAINS'. One slight breeze and the stack would crumble, sending you back to the start of the game.

As player after player around him fell, Simon emerged victorious – and immediately rushed to celebrate with Shaun, the rugged seven-foot-tall former AFL player who Simon desperately wanted to impress. That's nice and all, except that Shaun was meant to be one of our enemies, the leader of the minority alliance working against us. What was even worse, Shaun couldn't take the smile off his face. They were having the most genuine natural responses of celebration you could ever see. At one stage, Simon even jumped into his arms and Shaun was holding him up like one of his kids.

It was a joyous moment, for sure. But here I was, thinking … Why aren't you celebrating with your alliance, Simon?

Those moments of weakness – celebration, anger, the times when emotion takes over – are when you should keep a close eye on the people you're trying to read. They'll tell you everything you need to know. Simon gave his hand away and confirmed what my instincts were telling me: that he had flipped loyalties.

When we got back to camp, Simon tried to walk his reaction back, cosying up to me. What I didn't know at the

THOSE MOMENTS OF WEAKNESS – CELEBRATION, ANGER, THE TIMES WHEN EMOTION TAKES OVER – ARE WHEN YOU SHOULD KEEP A CLOSE EYE ON THE PEOPLE YOU'RE TRYING TO READ.

time was that the minority alliance of three – Shaun, Sam and Nina Twine – had two immunity idols between them. But what Simon didn't know is that I had already worked out his plan to blindside me from his body language. Using this information, in a night where I had a one in three chance of my torch being snuffed, I managed to flush both idols and send Sam home in an epic blindside. Maybe the only worse thing than being sent home with two hidden immunity idols in your pocket is playing two of them and not saving anyone at all.

That night, Simon's body language told me everything I needed to know. He had walked the plank all by himself.

PART 3

GLORY OR DEATH

WHAT TO DO WITH YOUR THRONE ONCE YOU HAVE TAKEN IT

CHAPTER 16

CELEBRATE YOUR OWN WINS

No, it's not a birthmark. Or a sticker. And no, it doesn't come off in the wash.

Who knew one little (well, not so little) tattoo could be so controversial?

I never had a tattoo before my first season of *Survivor* – now I have four, and they're all tributes to the game I love so much.

It started as a bonding experience with Dani Beale, a strong former prison guard on my first season of *Survivor* in Outback Queensland. I really liked Dani, but I just couldn't get her to like me. It happens in *Survivor*: one misunderstanding or bad impression and a player can write you off for the whole game. You usually have to wait until afterwards, when you're away from the cameras and the show ends, to try to reapproach the relationship without so much at stake (which is exactly what we did – I love Dani to bits, went to her surprise engagement and have even hung out with her very cool mum).

One night with probably just over a week left in the game, lying out in the dirt under the stars and hoping we weren't about to get bitten by a snake, Dani told me about all her many tattoos, and I decided I was going to get one. To me, tattoos had always been a big commitment. Getting something permanently marked onto your skin? You'd have to be really sure about it. But now here I was on *Survivor*, probably the thing I'd been most sure about in my entire life. It seemed logical that I take the plunge and make my first tattoo an ode to the game I loved so much.

So the day after I arrived back home from Cloncurry, I got my first tattoo: a green fire emoji, yellow brain emoji and red crown on my right forearm positioned like a triangle. These symbolised my two tribes and their colours as well as the crown that would be with me forever, whether I had won or lost (we didn't know at the time for sure!).

My tattooist in Bankstown, Lee, was fascinated why the brain was yellow and the fire green. I just said, 'Because it is!', not giving any content away as the season had not aired yet. He thought I was trying to set a new emoji trend.

For me, tattoos represent confidence. They are with you forever and are a public display of who you love and what you are proud of. This is why people tattoo names of their kids on their biceps and portraits of pets on their calves. I don't have kids, and I already had my dog, Douglas, immortalised on a Hawaiian shirt. But I do have something else I am particularly proud of that I carry in my heart everywhere I go.

As I was preparing to leave for Samoa in May 2022, I had an idea: what if I got my hidden immunity idol tattooed on my chest, just like the way I wore it on the Brains tribe?

Crazy. Random. But it was an opportunity for me to immortalise a moment when I felt on top of the world, my best version of myself, and frankly – Lee the tattooist thought it would look *sick*. And sick was how I felt, seven hours later, when it was finally done. Turns out, your sternum and collarbones are among the most painful places on your body to get tattooed. The skin is thinner, so the needle just about touches bone. I had a couple of shots of whisky at the six-hour mark, just to be able to see it through to the end.

It wasn't just the immunity necklace that I was proud of – it was how I had found it, and how I used it. We'd just lost a challenge to the other team. We returned to camp facing the reality that we'd soon be heading to tribal council to vote out one of our own.

This post-defeat moment has never been one of my favourite elements of *Survivor*: the tribe assembles for the routine post-loss Kumbayah moment, and then you get to business. The Brains tribe at the time had a toxic atmosphere. I didn't know that my alliance was being called the misfits, but we could definitely feel the animosity. I knew that this was a golden opportunity – and perhaps the *last* opportunity – to cause the level of chaos needed to change the status quo. If I didn't, they would have undoubtedly voted me out of my minority alliance of misfits.

I had the perfect plan. Little did my tribe know that I was in possession of a hidden immunity idol: I'd found it a few days earlier, hanging down from the branch of a tree, and I couldn't believe my luck. *Thank you, Macedonian Jesus,* I said to myself, tucking it into my pants and racing back to camp. I had kept the idol a secret from everybody except Cara, Baden and Wai at that stage, my close allies politically on the bottom of the tribe.

At this point, I knew I needed to cut some sort of deal. It was time for me to show my cards so that my fellow players would know I wasn't going anywhere – at least not during this tribal council.

I NEEDED TO CAUSE DYSFUNCTION. TRUE CHAOS.

They all needed to know that I was safe and that the pressure of the situation would strain personal relationships to the point where I could pick up the pieces and shift the priority from 'tribe strength' to political unity.

Having beat around the bush to find my idol, I knew there should be no beating around the bush when it came to playing it. I decided on the way back to camp from the failed immunity challenge that I would show everybody in camp exactly what I had, very, very publicly. As everyone stood around chatting, I moved to the back of the camp and retrieved the idol from its hiding place in the bottom of my bag. I swung it proudly around my neck and paraded back into camp, bare-chested, hands on hips. The King had arrived for the banquet of rice and nuts!

I carried on talking about anything but the idol; I figured I'd let the elephant in the room trumpet for itself. I could see everyone's faces fall, the cogs turning as they realised I wouldn't be going home that night, and they'd have to scramble for a Plan B.

And it wasn't just my tribemates who were agape. I will never forget the look on some of the producers' faces. In *Survivor*, the producers and the camera crew are like ghosts drifting in the background; they don't speak to you and you can't speak to them (unless summoned to film a confessional). But I caught the eye of one of them as I was ruffling through my bag behind the Brains shelter, put on my idol and proceeded to strut into camp with my it draped around my chest like a ticking time bomb. The producer's face was a mixture of shock and delight – and that was her trying *not* to show emotion!

What players traditionally do if they have an idol is reveal it last-minute at tribal council, or use it as a piece of behind-the-scenes strategy with their allies. Even though it takes the form of a necklace, only one person on *Australian Survivor*, Russell Hantz, had publicly worn it as one. But to me he was all bravado and no gameplay, and ended up having his torch snuffed with the idol around his neck.

Having that idol swinging around my bare chest was one of the best feelings of my life. As you now know, I had sweated it out before going to Cloncurry – and it was worth it. I remember wearing my idol at that tribal council and JLP remarked that I seemed to be pretty happy with how I looked. I was!

But one of my less friendly tribemates turned back to me, scowling. 'George's body is disgusting,' they hissed. This bit didn't make the edit, but I wish it had. Because anyone looking at the glow emanating from me in that moment would have known they were wrong.

My hidden immunity idol chest tattoo is a celebration. Of myself, my successes and my body, especially after how hard I'd worked to whip myself into shape to make it on to *Survivor*. It was important to me that I did it.

IF YOU DON'T CELEBRATE YOUR OWN ACHIEVEMENTS, WHO ELSE WILL?

(Plus, for any men reading, I think tattoos are hot.)

I kept the tattoo a secret for a while after I got it; no shirtless social media selfies or anything like that. Eventually, as I was doing the routine preparation with the producers for my second season of *Survivor*, I sent in the photos of me wearing my intended wardrobe for approval: including one in my purple villain undies, tattoo proudly on show. I received a call a few minutes later.

'George, we're all screaming in the office,' the producer bellowed. 'Is this legit? Is this a real tattoo? Did you really do this?'

I did, and kept it covered up right until the first episode of my second season. As JLP re-introduced me to my fellow players, I unbuttoned my shirt and let everyone bask in my new ink. It felt like such a baller moment, using my body to psych out my opponents: *Think you're the star of* Australian Survivor? *Check out THIS. My game. My Kingdom!*

Back at camp, my fellow players were full of questions – mostly the same ones the show's producers had asked. 'Yes, it's real,' I had to explain more than a few times. What did they think – that I'd painted it on just to make a grand entrance? What sort of industrial-grade lacquer was I possibly using to keep it from running into the South Pacific Ocean?

The internet loved asking me about it, too – or rather, shit-canning it. I keep an eye on social media, and I know some *Survivor* fans think my chest ink is one for the Bad Survivor Tattoo Hall of Fame. 'I want to take a cheese grater to George's body,' was one that made me laugh. Others were less inventive: 'That is the UGLIEST tattoo I've ever seen,' tweeted one viewer. 'George should get that HIDEOUS tattoo removed,' said another.

But I don't care. I love it. It's phenomenal. And guess who else loves it? Jonathan LaPaglia. Is there a bigger *Survivor* tattoo endorsement than that?

When people tell me my big old idol chest tattoo looks 'hideous', I have news for them: that's what the idol looked like. Please direct all complaints to *Australian Survivor*'s art department. If people think it's repulsive, or it looks ugly, or it looks like a broken heart or a claw, well, that's what it was. It's my idol. And I'm so proud of it.

Here's what many people don't realise: that chest tattoo is actually a cover-up. Shortly before I went on my first *Survivor* season, I developed a small cyst square in the middle of my chest, right on my sternum. I went to the doctor to have it removed and, well, doctors in Bankstown can be a bit rough and ready, and in the process of removing it, my small cyst was replaced by a much bigger keloid scar. Great. About to make my TV debut running around the Outback with my shirt off, and I suddenly have what looks like a big, bumpy third nipple smack back in the middle of my chest? Great.

Viewers noticed it, and I hated it. Covered it up with an idol tattoo, and I loved it!

But as anybody with parents born overseas can attest, the disapproval of strangers is nothing compared to the cold glare you get from an ethnic parent when you show them you've got a tattoo. My mum had the same response to all my tattoos: a sigh, a head shake, and the question: 'What's your father going to think?' Well, regardless of what he thinks, he's never actually said anything about them, positive or negative. But I think both my parents are quite happy going through life pretending their son doesn't have *Survivor*-themed tattoos adorning his body.

It's also made for some interesting reactions in other situations where a person would take their shirt off, if you get my drift. Sometimes I forget that there's a whole, rather large, portion of the world out there who aren't *Survivor* nerds. I've had one or two *what on earth is that?* reactions in the heat of the moment. ('It's an idol … it protects me when I need saving,' is my go-to sexily mysterious response. Best not to ruin the moment by describing the intricacies of *Survivor* gameplay.)

But my chest tat isn't my only *Survivor* body art. I found another idol in my second season, and this time I decided to permanently put it on my hand. I promised I'd get a tattoo of it during filming, and I always keep my promises. After filming had wrapped, I called the show's production team and asked them to send me a photo of the idol, as I wanted my tattooist to copy the design. They rang me back pretty swiftly and asked if I was sure I really wanted another *Survivor* idol tattoo.

'Not only am I going to do it,' I told them, my tone turning as icy as those early Samoan mornings on the beach, 'I'm also not asking *for your permission.*'

They gave me the image of the idol – and I gave the video of the tattooing process to Network Ten. Their post about it became the most-watched online video of the season – including more views than when my friend Olympian Liz Parnov was crowned the winner! It even got a *TV Week* spread.

I now even have matching Heroes v Villains emoji tattoos on my left forearm: purple devil emoji, yellow hero emoji, and the merge logo of the other tribe I named, Mole Mole.

(Fun fact: When I was on fentanyl in the Samoan hospital, I remember there being a sign in Samoan that had the word 'fa'amolemole'. This means both 'please' and 'I'm hungry', as I was told by the fixer by my bedside. Fentanyl George's mind went to *Austin Powers*, and the infamous 'mole mole mole mole mole' scene from *Goldmember,* and I started laughing. When it came to naming the merged tribe of heroes and villains, the first suggestion was 'Camilla', in honour of then-Prince Charles's long-term lover and the perfect hero/villain combo. This was quickly shut down by Hayley (we didn't know she was technically our Queen at that stage) so I thought back to 'Mole Mole'. I thought naming the tribe 'I'm hungry' in Samoan was funny, but if people think it's an *Austin Powers* reference, then good for them!)

Every time I look at my tattoos, I think of some of the happiest moments of my life. To me, they're a way to honour my achievements. You don't have to be as extreme as me –

NOT EVERY MILESTONE NEEDS SEVEN HOURS IN A TATTOOIST'S CHAIR AND A FEW SHOTS OF WHISKY – BUT YOU HAVE TO CELEBRATE YOUR OWN WINS IN SOME SHAPE OR FORM.

Now, I know what some of you might be thinking: *George … you DIDN'T win* Survivor. Maybe I didn't walk away with the $500k, but I left a legacy that will be spoken about forever, and that is priceless. To me, that is more valuable than the win, and it's worth celebrating.

RALLY YOUR TROOPS LIKE YOU'VE JUST WON A BATTLE AND IT'LL NOT ONLY SCARE OFF THE NAYSAYERS – IT'LL BANISH THOSE LITTLE NIGGLING VOICES INSIDE YOU, TOO.

I celebrate my wins in more private ways, too. If you ever get an invite to King George's palace, you'll spy something of a *Survivor* shrine in my bedroom. It takes up a bookshelf and whole wall at the foot of my bed, so it's the first thing I see when I wake up and the last thing I see before I go to bed. My Buffs are there – still caked in dirt and sweat – and I lovingly framed the idol clues I found through my seasons like ancient parchments. There are my letters from home, some photos from the show, and even one of my immunity idols, returned to its rightful owner after the season ended. It all serves as a daily visual reminder of one of my proudest achievements in life.

So I challenge you to channel your inner King George when you reach those personal milestones in life. Aced that job interview? Landed that pay rise? Smashed that 10 kilometre run? Shout it from the rooftops and celebrate! Not always with some ink, but loudly enough that all your enemies know. Rally your troops like you've just won a battle and it'll not only scare off the naysayers – it'll banish those little niggling voices inside you, too.

Is that arrogance? Arrogance is unearned confidence. You have earned every reason to be confident. So wear it loud and proud on your chest – I know I do.

WHEN LIFE GIVES YOU LEMONADE, PACKAGE IT AND SELL IT

I know what you probably think life's like for an ex-*Australian Survivor* contestant. Podcast tapings, TV appearances, regular reunions at Jonathan LaPaglia's mansion while we wait for him to finish his bicep curls and join us for lunch?

For the most part, yes. Sadly not the bit about JLP, though – although his mother-in-law is a fan, and once invited me to her house for sandwiches. (I'm yet to take her up on the offer.)

But here's what nobody tells you about achieving reality-TV-contestant-level fame: you'll suddenly have a lot of people sliding into your DMs asking for favours.

'My mum loves you,' someone will write. 'Can you please wish her a happy birthday?'

'My uncle is your biggest fan,' says another. 'Can you please wish him good luck in his divorce?'

'My dog howls every time you appear on screen,' comes another request. 'Can you please tell him to take his worming tablets?'

You have a few options in this situation. You could ignore the requests and forever be known as 'that arsehole off the TV'. You could respond to each and every one out of the kindness of your heart, getting diddly squat in return. Or you could join Cameo.

Cameo is a video messaging service populated by celebrities and sportspeople from throughout the world where you can pay a small fee to them to record a personalised message for you. With so many reality shows airing at any moment, it is a flooded market. Do you remember who went home first on the last season of *The Bachelor*? No? Well, for the right price, you can receive a personalised video message from them. Tempting, no?

I've carved out quite the niche for myself in this flooded Cameo market.

On a platform that has thousands of reality stars and other celebrities jostling to get your attention, I am the top Australian. Me! By volume, I regularly rank among the top 50 creators worldwide, and when this data came out, I was both surprised and proud.

I have never taken for granted that the audiences watching the shows I am on are the most important stakeholders in my career. What they think matters. How engaged they are with the show on social media matters. I want to make sure that the audiences watching *Survivor*, *The Amazing Race* and whatever comes next are invested in the show: through my actions while I'm playing the game, and then once I've left, through debate on social media.

I went onto my first reality-TV show with the attitude that I would be received with both open arms and pitchforks probably equally. What took me by surprise, and what I am grateful for, is how positively the audience responded to me being my authentic self.

I knew that I wanted to be myself the day I walked in, and every day after that. It's what I said in my audition process: with me, you take what you get. I'm a bit like hot sauce. Some people love their mouths igniting with fire, some will never go near it because they don't like the burn and some like a little dash of chilli oil to spice up their lives.

On my first season of *Survivor*, rather than a 50:50 split, it was 80 per cent extreme love, 20 per cent extreme hate, and literally nobody without an opinion. This far exceeded even my greatest expectations, but also told me what people were fascinated by is what worked to get me on the show in the first place: being me.

George, a 34-year-old guy from Bankstown and proud of it, with a body on TV that reflects 80 per cent of men, and an interesting career history that's defining my *Survivor* character and gameplay. I am not one for the fake personas that people like to portray of their lives on social media. My brand is my personality, my life story, and everyday people can some way identify with that. And it's easy to deliver on your brand when you're just delivering yourself.

Which brings me back to Cameo. Being the number-one Australian on Cameo is something I worked hard for. It is all good and well knowing my brand and dishing it out, but I have always treated my engagement with my fans as if they were constituents in a marginal campaign seat. Every single interaction you have with your voters is critical. It *has* to be

IT'S EASY TO DELIVER ON YOUR BRAND WHEN YOU'RE JUST DELIVERING YOURSELF.

a 9/10 at minimum, because a positive experience will lead to good word of mouth, and this is how swing or undecided voters become locked-in voters. (Not that anyone is ever unsure about me – I know I'm a decisive, divisive guy.)

This was my approach to fan engagement. Every single time I have a random member of the public come up and speak to me, whether I am at the shops, eating lunch, on public transport, out and about in town or walking the streets of Bankstown, I try to give that fan an upbeat experience of me. I always say yes to the selfie – but not the video, you have to pay for that on Cameo – because it makes the fan happy. Happy fans, happy voters.

I'm grateful for this, so I take it seriously. The Cameo requests roll in daily. The requests range from birthday and anniversary well wishes to pep talks and an array of random message requests for fans of *Survivor* and *The Amazing Race*.

Filming Cameos is time consuming and I spend a good hour a day making them – it's not like sending off a quick voice note to a friend. People pay good money for them, and they expect a quality experience, so I always tailor my response to the message and instructions they give me. When I nail that brief, it's a win-win.

Every time I film one, I tell myself, *I need to make this an extremely engaging experience for my fan.* This must be the moment that really solidifies them as someone on my team, rather than the moment they go off me. If they get a laugh out of me, they'll tell their friends, they'll put it on their *Survivor* or *Amazing Race* group chat and then that generates more business and more interest in me. So I *have* to be excited. Book a message from me and you'll get the full King George experience: Want me to yell GLORY OR DEATH at your dear old nanna? I'll do it! If that is want from me, then that's exactly what I'll be doing.

If you are fortunate enough to experience the upside that reality-TV celebrity brings to your life like I have – I quit my old job as a public servant, continue to work in TV, and thank you for buying this book – then you should never forget how you got there in the first place. There was a community who were originally interested in and liked you, and you need to consider them as your number-one fans.

One moment that really locked this into my mind was when I was in Melbourne promoting Channel 10 at an Oz Comic-Con Convention. I was walking in the streets with a celebrity who had been on TV and I had been stopped four times in a 500-metre stretch to be asked for a selfie. I posed for photos, answered a few *Survivor*-related questions and then continued my way to the venue.

After the fourth time, the other celebrity looked at me judgementally. 'Why are you even stopping and talking to these nobodies?' they asked, sneering.

It was an easy response for me: 'Because these fans pay my bills. Making them happy is important to me.'

I think about that interaction a lot, because it reminds me what made my brand in the first instance: me being me.

IN TRUTH, I BRISTLE A BIT AT DESCRIBING MYSELF AS A 'BRAND'. IT SUGGESTS SOMETHING FAKE, A PERSONA PUT ON FOR THE CAMERAS. HERE'S ONE THING SOME PEOPLE STILL STRUGGLE TO UNDERSTAND ABOUT ME: *I'M LIKE THIS ALL THE TIME.*

People call me the King each and every day on the street, but what you saw on TV is what you get. This is actually how I am when I am out and about with Mike and Stevie on a Saturday night. Pub-crawl George.

It's why I can get away with sometimes being a bit shameless with my sponsored content and online product placement. My followers like to see me win. If a guy from Western Sydney can make it, it gives people hope that they can, too.

I remember thinking about how I'd approach my second season differently to my first. There were mistakes I wanted to correct, obviously, none more so than the optics of my perceived lack of a physical game. But one thing I knew I wouldn't change was my personality. *If it ain't broke, don't fix it,* I thought. King George made a splash first time around, so let's do it again.

Of course, it doesn't come naturally for everyone in the world to swing an immunity idol around their head screaming *GLORY OR DEATH!* on international TV. For a lot of people, simply 'being yourself' in situations might mean you fade into the background and struggle to stand out. There's nothing *wrong* with this – introverts and quiet people are an important part of the social fabric, even though they don't always make for great TV. If you do desire to get your mug on the screen though, or even just be noticed at parties, this is where you can take a bit more creative licence. You can decide exactly what you'd like your personal brand to be and craft it from the ground up. What would you like your peers to know you for? How would you want them to describe you? If you can name a few attributes, you can start focusing on exhibiting them in your interactions with people.

Would you like to be known as a generous person? Start with some simple acts of kindness – they go a long way to quickly building trust. Something as simple as buying your workmate a coffee in the morning can start to build that new interpretation of your personality for them. Remember though, this is all just about appearances and optics. They don't need to know it was the free coffee you got with your completed stamp card at the local café. Just make sure you *absolutely insist* they don't pay you back for that (free) coffee.

How about hardworking? Everyone wants to make their boss think they're the most dedicated worker in the office. One simple shortcut is making sure you regularly start work early or stay late. That may sound like a drag, but here's a little secret: you don't actually have to be doing work for all that time. You could stay in the office until 6:30pm but be booking your next holiday. What people will remember is when you got into work and when you left. Perception is reality and it'll appear that you put in more work than others around you.

Humour is an easy one. Just about everyone wants to be thought of as funny. There are so many shortcuts here – Google is your friend, so search for jokes and memorise a few. The key is to not appear like you're trying too hard: interjecting in a social situation to recite a dutifully memorised joke can come off as desperate. Better to say, 'I heard the funniest joke last night, want to hear it?' Again, over time people will forget that you set it up as someone else's joke – they'll just remember laughing at it. A few of those, and you'll be known as the funny guy in the office with the mental Rolodex of jokes.

All of this requires a degree of self-examination. It requires you identifying your weaknesses and committing to work on them.

SO MANY PEOPLE SHY AWAY FROM SELF-AWARENESS. THAT'S BECAUSE MOST PEOPLE DON'T REALLY LIKE INTERROGATING THEMSELVES – ESPECIALLY THEIR FLAWS. BUT IF YOU GET INTO THE HABIT OF DOING IT FOR YOURSELF, YOU'LL GIVE YOURSELF A BIG ADVANTAGE.

I have the proof: the success I'm experiencing with Cameo is a result of years of honing my personality and trimming away what doesn't serve me. Don't get me wrong, I am truly 'myself' and I always have been, but I've cast aside the less successful aspects of my personality – the nerves, the self-doubt – to focus on the winning ones.

But you have to know your limits. To paraphrase Meat Loaf: I will do anything for Cameo, but I won't do that. One person repeatedly requested I make a Cameo saying anti-Semitic remarks, a request I kept rejecting – and they kept re-submitting. Now *that's* off-brand. (And besides, there's gotta be better ways to spend your $55.)

The only other request I considered denying was after my first season of *Survivor*, when the producers were really honing-in on the political operative narrative of my life experience. There was a State by-election happening in the North Shore electorate, and a Liberal staff member asked me to give advice to Tim James, a Liberal candidate, on how to run a political operation and make people do what you want. It was a slippery request: I was all over the television as a then-member of the Labor party – should I shill for the other side for the princely sum of $55?

Did I do it? Of *course* I did. I took that Liberal party dude's $55 and I recorded a targeted political-advice message without saying the words Liberal, Tim James or North Shore. He got a positive customer experience, and I managed not to spout anything that could be used against me as the Bankstown Labor President.

IT'S A CROWDED MARKET OUT THERE – IN THE JOB MARKET, THE RENTAL MARKET AND EVEN THE DATING MARKET. KNOWING YOUR OWN PERSONAL BRAND CAN HELP YOU STAND OUT WHERE OTHERS BLEND INTO THE BACKGROUND.

If you want to be memorable, work on bringing out the aspects of your personality you want people to focus on, and make them your *thing*. If you do, you'll not only be living true to your values – it'll lead to a higher success rate in whatever market you're shopping around in.

And if you're still a little lost about what your personal brand is, King George hereby grants you permission to steal a bit of his! Be brash, be clever, be confident. Just don't go getting a giant idol tattoo on your chest, or you'll be hearing from my lawyer – who happens to be me!

CHAPTER 18

KNOW WHEN TO RELINQUISH YOUR POWER

I've spoken a lot in this book about how I've been able to get ahead in life by controlling those around me. But I have a confession to make: in truth, there's one situation, one relationship, where I find myself constantly hamstrung by someone who *always* gets their way. Try as I might, I'm wrapped around their little finger (well, toe).

His name's Douglas. And he's a small, fluffy, needy Maltese terrier.

I had always wanted a dog growing up but never had the opportunity to have one. That was up until I started renting my own apartment in Bankstown. Sometimes I would drive past the RSPCA and look at the dogs for adoption, and I would also regularly scan online classifieds. Doug was from such an ad. A backyard breeder in a housing commission property was selling him, and at the time he was tiny and frail: just four weeks old, and also quite sick as he'd had no veterinary care. I had no intention of buying him until I held him in my arms, and after that, I immediately took him. With Doug, it was love at first sight.

But he can be naughty. Doug is definitely a villain and master manipulator. He loves to get his way and rarely takes no for an answer. He likes to lure me into a false sense of security with his sweet-looking eyes, particularly when I'm eating, and then he will pounce and snap up my dinner from under my fork. Doug loves food, particularly human food, and if I want to eat it, so does he. As a result, Dougie *runs* my house, especially at mealtimes.

It's become a bit of a problem – which you'll already know if you happened to catch our episode of the Channel 10 show *Dogs Behaving (Very) Badly*. King George from *Survivor* went out the window during that particular TV appearance. Suddenly, viewers saw a very different side of me: as a loyal servant to one very pampered, hungry pooch. Dog training expert Graeme Hall did his best to shift the dynamic, but in truth, I think both Douglas and I prefer things the way they were.

That's because spending your days holding court can become tiring. Seizing power and keeping it is a draining exercise, so it's important to have places in your life where you can let your guard down a little. Let someone else lead – literally, in the case of this seven-kilo terrier, who consistently drags me around the block on his leash. Without Douglas in my life, I wouldn't have a safe, comforting space to retreat to on the hard days, which is probably why I let him get away with everything he does.

After all, pets are the ultimate masters of winning friends and manipulating people. They know they can get away with nearly anything they want. Reduce the arm of your favourite sofa to confetti? That can be solved by adopting an adorably guilty expression. Eat an entire loaf of Turkish bread while you were in the bathroom? All is forgiven with an affectionate lick of the nose. Beyond a tug on the collar or the denial of treats, there are rarely ever many consequences to their naughty deeds.

Instead, we go out of our way to make sacrifices for them. We shower them with endless novelty presents, pay more for their haircuts than I do at my local barber in Bankstown, and organise our holidays around sitter schedules. It is a time-consuming and expensive exercise, yet we love them all the more for it. (Any pet owner who has had their animal swallow a piece of string and seen the vet bill afterwards will know what I'm talking about.) Despite all his neuroticisms, I wear my love for Douglas on my sleeve – literally, in the case of the two shirts I made with his face on them to wear in my *Survivor* seasons. (I later auctioned those shirts for charity, so he really is a good boy.)

There's a lot we can learn from our pets about commanding love, committing soft-toy murder and then getting away with it. But what I've learned from Dougie is that everyone needs to have one kingdom in which you are not the ruler. By being reminded that you are not always the one with the power, you can learn from the best, conserve your energy and then go back out into the world ready to seize it by the scruff of its neck.

CHAPTER 19

FIGHT FIRE WITH FIRE

There are some common words of wisdom you might be used to hearing from people in the public eye: Don't feed the trolls. Ignore the haters. Turn the other cheek.

Where's the fun in that?

Something interesting happens when you're beamed into people's living rooms multiple nights a week for several months. People have opinions about you – and they feel it's their duty to voice them publicly.

Survivor and *The Amazing Race* fans can be brutal – I should know, I am one. Make one wrong move, or stick around longer than someone's favourite player, and in their eyes you can be a dead man walking.

I know I'm a bit like Vegemite – some people love me,

others hate me. That's fine by me. At least I'm not a bland piece of white toast! Do you know how memorable you have to be to inspire a legion of haters? So many *Survivor* contestants are all-but-forgotten by the time their torches are snuffed, or drop out of our minds before they drop out of the Race. I've sent more than a couple home, and I've just about forgotten their names by the time we've made it back to camp or the next pit stop. Remember that doctor dude from the Outback or the beauty queen from Samoa? Neither did I until I googled my *Survivor* castmates and it triggered something in the deep recess of my memory.

Some reality-TV contestants get so wrapped up in the negative comments you'd think every random tweet bagging them was a handwritten note from their mum in their lunchbox, the way they take it to heart. Some 14-year-old hiding under an anonymous account calling you names should not be cause for a breakdown.

ME? I SAY COME AT ME – AND I'LL RETURN FIRE.

I do this for a few reasons. It is against expert advice. Rule number one for anyone on TV is 'don't read the comments', but a lot of keyboard warriors seem to have forgotten that it's a human being they're dissing. Sometimes it's good to remind people that you're there and that you can see what they're saying – and it's so goddamn satisfying sometimes to put them in their place.

I had so much fun with this on my second go at *Survivor*, ignoring all the expert advice to stay off social media.

IGNORE IT? I WALLOWED IN IT LIKE A PIG IN MUD! YOU COME FOR KING GEORGE, YOU BEST COME CORRECT.

It's a philosophy that carries over into the real world, too. So many people avoid confrontation, even when it's warranted. Someone at work or school shit-canning you behind your back? CALL. THEM. OUT. Take back your power. You'd be surprised how often the person doing the shit-talking is mortified to be confronted about it. (Case in point: most of the people I clap back on Twitter delete their tweets – and sometimes their whole accounts – shortly after I respond.)

If you're wondering why I'm so unfazed by social media trolls while some other people in the public eye schedule a tearful press conference every time they read a bad tweet, I think I know the answer: a lot of these celebrities have never had an actual job.

Real jobs mean real people, and a lot of the time, real people are just not very nice. Let me tell you about my first job, back when I was in high school. I worked in a call centre, cold-calling people to sell them lottery tickets. It wasn't a scam, it was for Vision Australia (a charity that supports people who are blind), but it sure sounded like one to most people, as this teenager asked them to provide their credit card details for the chance to win big prizes.

I was good at it – a smooth operator, even as a teen – but can you imagine the abuse I copped? I mean, I had every insult under the sun slung at me by drunk people sitting on their sofa. For every time I'd close a sale, there would be countless people hanging up after berating me for calling them during dinner, or *Neighbours*, or their dog's nightly bath.

After that I worked the checkout at Bankstown Kmart and, later, taking people's bets at PhoneTAB. All public-facing jobs, all with ample opportunity for abuse from the general public. (Yes, even Kmart – stressed mums doing the Christmas shopping rush can definitely have a nasty streak.) And throughout it all, I had to smile and take it. 'Thank you, have a nice day' and all that.

Now I don't. Send me abuse, I can hit you right back. Those years in thankless, customer-facing jobs trained me to cop abuse without any fuss. But nowadays, I don't have to stay silent anymore.

And besides, when you're dealing with haters, the best thing you can do is confront them and put the attention back on them. Usually when you do that, they melt away. They thrive in the dark – they can't handle the glare of the spotlight.

Think you can do better? I'm at @KingGeorge2200. Hit me with your best shot.

CHAPTER 20

USE ALL OF THESE TOOLS TO RULE LIKE A GLORIOUS KING

There are many aspects of my life that I am proud of. One of them is being the first person in four generations of my family to complete a university degree. For 100 years, people in my family lived through upheaval, dispossession and war, which prevented them from being able to have basic rights like access to education to enrich their lives. Australia eventually provided the stability and opportunity my family needed in the mid-20th century, and it eventually bore fruit with me.

Another aspect I'm proud of is all the work and the little wins I was able to achieve in fighting to improve the lives of the people in Bankstown, especially when I worked with

Tania Mihailuk and was a Bankstown Labor official. Tania was an incredible mentor and friend to me, and she instilled in me the fortitude to continually fight for what's needed, even when the odds are stacked against you. I did everything I could to weed out corruption and to stop the neglect of an area usually ignored by different levels of government. There's still work to be done to fix Bankstown so it can reach its potential, but I'm proud of what I have contributed to the cause so far.

But one achievement that I'm just as proud of is a legendary moment that played out in front of a national TV audience. This was in Episode Seven of *Australian Survivor: Heroes v Villains*, and is now remembered globally in only three words: 'best tribal ever'.

On *Survivor*, tribal council is judgement day. It is the moment where in front of your peers, and sometimes a jury, the trials and tribulations of the days and weeks that have passed by come to a boiling point. At the end of it, one unlucky person has their life in the game, in the form of a torch, snuffed.

Plans, alliances and loyalty get tested. The pressure is real, panic sets in, some people flounder and others shine. During this particular tribal, over the course of what was 40 straight minutes of TV footage and several hours in real life, I solidified friendships, tested and destroyed others, made new enemies and flipped a tricky situation to become the best-case scenario for me despite it being inherently designed to destroy me.

It was the ultimate example of how to win friends and manipulate people. For me, every single tip in this book was put into action on that one night, and that tribal council showdown became more valuable and important to me than actually winning the game. This book is the packaged-up version of how I won friends and manipulated people at that tribal council, and the perfect way to help illustrate everything you have learned.

Now, to explain how I was able to pull it all off.

When the game started on Day One, the Villains tribe was split evenly with six returning players – myself, Shonee, Simon, Jordie, Jackie and Stevey – and six new players. Playing *Survivor* more than once with other returning players is difficult, because in one way or another, there are always outside dynamics and relationships that can influence what happens inside of the game.

Jordie was the most recent returning player, with his Blood v Water season having recently finished airing on Channel 10. I tend to call things as I see them. I was one of the most publicly vociferous critics of Jordie's 'man only' alliance in Blood v Water, and his 'mateship/bros first' mindset. Jordie knew that, and I believed that he resented it.

About a month before we travelled to Samoa, I had seen on social media that Jordie had been socialising with Simon, a returning player from my original Brains v Brawn season. I knew this would not be good for me, because while I had no official confirmation of which players would be returning for a second time, I knew if Jordie was meeting with Simon, who had been blaming me for his vote off with two idols in Brains v Brawn, the purpose of that meeting would be to form a pre-game alliance against me in Samoa.

Then a few days before we flew to Samoa, Simon called me. I knew he had spoken to at least 50 past *Survivor* players about playing again, but this was the first time he was making contact with me. Highly suspicious. I just played dumb and let him do all the talking.

Simon said he missed me. Simon said he couldn't wait to work with me on the Villains tribe. Simon said he would be waving at Brisbane airport.

I immediately suspected that Simon, along with Jordie, was going to target me the moment we stepped off the truck and onto the mat in front of JLP. He was hoping I would let my guard down, but I stayed cordial.

'Thanks, Simo,' I said fondly. 'I'm pumped. See you then.'

I can never sleep the night before the flight leaves for *Survivor*. In the end, I went down to the lobby at around 5am ahead of our 6am call, waiting to see which three Villains would be in my travel group to the airport. The first person to walk into the hotel lobby was Jackie. I couldn't be more delighted! I waved, she pulled down her facemask to flash a big smile, then went back into professional mode. Fantastic for me – an immediate friend.

A second returning player I was familiar with was Stevey. I had met him once before and I thought he was an interesting but completely left-field choice for a returning player. He was voted out in 21st place in Season Three and was known for his erratic and self-declared sneaky behaviour. I thought I could work with him, though: I knew that he was *very* passionate about *Survivor* and politics, which we both have in common.

The final returning player for me was Shonee, a complete enigma. Shonee is beloved by the *Survivor* fanbase and is an extremely good TV performer and confessionalist. I had never met Shonee prior to going to Samoa, but I suspected she was going to be on the Villains tribe. I had seen her post Instagram stories of her shopping for lilac clothing, and given I was also shopping for lilac clothing, I was expecting to see her at Brisbane airport.

While I had never spoken to Shonee beforehand, I knew that she either likes you or she doesn't, she's fiercely independent and she goes more off vibes rather than strategy. This gave me hope that if I got along with Shonee in camp and she saw me as 'one of her people', then she would want to work with me.

While I had some form of a relationship or familiarity with the returning villains, the six first-time players on the tribe were all unknowns. Fraser was one of them. I didn't have a clue who he was, but I did see his name tag on his suitcase at the airport. At this stage, production hadn't taken our phones away from us yet, so on a strategic toilet break, I furiously googled his name, made phone calls to multiple people I knew who followed his Instagram page and concluded he was just another Instagrammer. I immediately pigeonholed him as unthreatening.

While I hadn't met her before, I enjoyed watching Anjali when she hosted *Dateline* on SBS. The other newbies on the Villains tribe – Liz, Sarah, Mimi and Michael – were complete unknowns to me. So on Day One of the game, I had to extract as much information from them as possible in camp and then make judgement calls on their personalities, values and motivations as time went on.

Liz and I got along famously thanks to our shared Slavic

heritage. I could read her Russian Cyrillic tattoo, and she had a great personality. Michael I instantly didn't warm too, but luckily for me nobody else in camp did, either. Mimi kept her cards very close to her chest but I told myself I saw potential in her and we gelled. And Sarah? Well, she had never seen a second of *Survivor* previously, and I saw every returning player's eyes roll when she asked when we would be bussed to the hotel room on Night One after the sun had set. (Really.)

Prior to the accident where Jackie and I were injured, the two of us had worked tirelessly to discern the agenda and priorities of the Villains tribe. We were a trio with Anjali — a 25 per cent voting bloc at any future tribal council. We encouraged a truce with the returning players so we could pick off the newbies first. Jordie needed about five minutes in camp to start 'bro-ing' it up with Simon, which was making Liz uncomfortable and Shonee worried.

WHEN I RETURNED TO CAMP ON DAY THREE AFTER MY INJURY, I HAD LOST THE MOST VALUABLE *SURVIVOR* COMMODITIES: TIME AND ALLIES.

Jackie and Anjali were gone, decimating my initial alliance. Those early days for influencing players are crucial, and not only had I lost a whole one, but I was also 24 hours behind on what gossip had been bubbling. I did have a path to survival though, and I knew it was by befriending Shonee and Liz.

While Shonee is a big character on TV, in camp she actually plays the game of *Survivor* from a position of fear. Shonee was petrified of the fact that she would be targeted for being the first-ever third-time returning player. This was good for me, because while we were having conversations about oysters and margaritas, I would emphasise that if a 'big player' (me) went home next, it would cause a domino effect where we all went. It was a way to get her to protect me in order to protect herself.

At the same time, I was delighted by the fact that Jordie, Simon and Stevey had become a male trio, as predicted. Shonee knew that Stevey was resentful towards her, and Liz, as a strong woman, was not liking the way Simon spoke differently to the men and women in camp. I didn't even have to massage that situation – they were digging their own graves in the sand.

In the lead up to the Episode Seven tribal council, Michael and Sarah were sent home in straightforward votes. I also found a hidden immunity idol, which I kept a complete secret from every single person on my tribe. By that time, I was firmly locked into working with Shonee and Liz as part of the self-proclaimed 'Spice Girls' alliance.

Fraser's only true ally in the game was Mimi. By the end of the first week in the game, I had made one very important observation about Fraser that proved to be correct. As the son of a wealthy real-estate agent, who became a real-estate agent himself because that's what his father probably told him to do, I assumed that he was the kind of person who would do what they're told. If Fraser was drawn into the all-man alliance of Jordie and Simon, he would simply follow their instructions.

But then he lost my respect. The night Mimi was voted off, it was supposed to be Stevey. I got up on my feet at this tribal to try to save Mimi. I liked Mimi; she had a backbone. While I was championing her cause, I was asking myself: Why is Mimi's only friend, Fraser, sitting down, doing nothing, and looking to Simon and Jordie for direction?

Mimi went home, and after that tribal, Fraser was completely dead to me as an option of someone to work with in the game. Fraser was under zero threat at tribal councils, he barely spoke a word at camp and he could've tried to convince people to stick to voting for Stevey over his friend Mimi, but he did nothing.

In my mind, this was an active sign of his *Survivor* character. You do not want a player like Fraser, who digs their head in the sand and hides when something goes wrong in the game. I did not want to risk having Fraser in the game and being in a minority position in a tribe swap.

AUSTRALIAN SURVIVOR HISTORY HAS SHOWN THAT UNDER-THE-RADAR PLAYERS WHO DO LITTLE IN THE GAME ALWAYS GET TO THE END, BECAUSE NOBODY EVER SEES THEM AS THREATENING ENOUGH TO VOTE OUT.

Once Mimi had gone home, Fraser was joined at the hip with Jordie and Simon in a bro alliance. In the week prior to the Episode Seven tribal council, I had begun winding Jordie up, playing off how I thought the public would perceive him. I suspected that Jordie would have read online commentary that called the male-only alliance he was a member of in Blood v Water as misogynistic. This was an important assumption to make, because Jordie was repeating past patterns this season. Earlier on, we had formed what was a genuine 'night chat' secret alliance to make sure we would both avoid becoming the target of our opposing alliances. I would tell Jordie regularly at night that the girls disliked how Simon had formed an all-man alliance and how he was speaking to them in camp. That's when Jordie realised that he had to detach himself from Simon.

Simon is a good person, but I think he's the kind of person who gets caught up in the heat of the moment. In Jordie, he saw the perfect mate, but the more that Simon spoke down to me, or shut down Liz and Shonee in conversations, I believe the more Jordie understood that the people watching *Survivor* at home would character assassinate him due to Simon's behaviour.

At camp the afternoon of that fateful tribal council, the tribe was split in Simon's bloc of four men and the three Spice Girls. To Simon, this was his golden moment to have all the men on the tribe, aside from me, vote me out. My plan was to reveal my hidden immunity idol to Shonee and Liz, play it, and then have our three minority votes send Simon packing in a blindside.

Fortunately for me, Jordie started feeling the cumulative pressure that I was putting on him. Jordie, the man who had been trying to end my game before it had even started, pulled Liz and I aside at camp. He told us that Simon had an immunity idol – we only discovered it was an insignificant piece of wood much later in the game – and that he wanted to vote Simon out to 'side with the girls'. Those late-night conversations I had with Jordie had finally paid off. He was ditching the boys club and wanted to change his ways! A miracle sent straight from Macedonian Jesus.

The ball started moving for blindsiding Simon and sending him home with an 'idol' – again. Late in the afternoon, Simon pulled me aside for a chat, the usual *Survivor* attempt to keep your target on-side by lying to their face. Simon is a horrifically terrible liar; I can hear his voice change. He told me he was voting for Stevey. A lie. Unbeknownst to him, with Fraser and Jordie having flipped to my side (I already knew that they were voting for him that tribal council), he'd thrown his only remaining ally in the game under the bus. I filed this information away to use against him later.

Meanwhile, I was doing my best to look scared. I had to let Simon believe that his plan to get rid of me looked like it was going to work. Shonee and Liz were acting like they would vote for me, and I went off for a fake search for an idol, which I already had.

I never like to close any door in life or in *Survivor*, and one of the last conversations I had before I pretended to stomp around the jungle was with Stevey. In his mind, Stevey thought he was stalling me in camp to stop me from looking for an idol, but we had a genuine heart to heart. He told me how much he respected me and wished he could work with me because I'm his favourite *Survivor* player – but in this game, we were just on different sides. My alliance was targeting his friend Simon, and in his mind there was nothing he could do.

Stevey is a very genuine and heartfelt kind of person, and I knew exactly where he stood. I respected that. I said to him that things between us might be different based on who woke up on the beach tomorrow.

Off to tribal council we went. From my perspective, the mission was simple. This was Jordie's move, his active choice to take control of his game and to not be thought of as a misogynist. I had to make sure to have the spotlight focused solely on Simon and goad him to speak down to me. If I could pull this off, Shonee and Liz would become uncomfortable, which would make Jordie uncomfortable, and further validate his decision to betray Simon because of the way Simon spoke to people in the game.

As I told Jonathan LaPaglia, the tribe would vote out a weak link tonight. Simon fell for my trap – hook, line and sinker.

'You can't vote for yourself,' he chided.

It was such a schoolboy taunt. I asked him what he meant, and he explained that I wasn't 'the strongest horse in the stable'.

'Thank you for pointing out that I'm weak,' I told him, keeping my tone calm and measured, to let the cruelty of his insult hang in the air. I could feel Jordie squirm.

And then came a huge twist that threw the Simon blindside out with the bathwater. Jonathan LaPaglia said that before we'd vote, we'd immediately do an elaborate fire-making challenge for the chance to win individual immunity.

This was a disaster as far as I was concerned – thanks, JLP. Simon would've been a short odds favourite to win a fire-based immunity challenge: he's a skilled tradie and regularly made fire back at camp. But I wasn't too rattled, because a) I still had my hidden immunity idol as a protectionist failsafe, and b) if Simon didn't win immunity, nothing would change in the blindside plan that Jordie had concocted.

As the challenge began, Simon immediately pulled ahead. As he did so, he felt the need to taunt my challenge record from the Outback. He thought he was being smug, and he was – but it only continued to anger Shonee and Liz.

Simon had broken away to a huge lead. He was skilled at the fire-making component, while Jordie couldn't tie his sticks together, and I had tied too many sticks together to grab a key. At this point, I had two options with my limited time: try to fix my sticks or set up a new plan. I used my time wisely.

While Simon was starting his fire, I walked up to Shonee and Liz and revealed that I had found an idol when I was looking, right before we left – a believable white lie about its origins – and I planned to play it. I suggested that we vote for Stevey, and Shonee and Liz agreed. I walked up to Jordie and he was immediately on board for Stevey. Fraser just nodded in silence as usual. Annoying.

Simon was oblivious to this going on, furiously making fire. As expected, he won immunity, putting on a fake cry of happiness for cameras while he was at it. Shortly after, the crew isolated the players from each other so that they could reset the cameras. This was a critical period of time for me, because it would be around 20 minutes before our tribe would walk back in and sit down in front of JLP again. That's a lot of time to think.

I had a decent plan ready to fire: play my idol, save myself, and let Stevey go home. But while we were walking back to tribal council, the realisation hit me. If Stevey went home as I initially had been contemplating, I would be putting myself in a 3-3 scenario: myself, Shonee and Liz against Jordie, Fraser and Simon. My instinct was telling me that if pushed, Shonee and Liz might flip and I would then go home in a 5-1 vote at the next Villains tribal council. King George knocked off his throne.

As our torches were handed back to us by the crew to walk into tribal council, I changed my plan. I no longer wanted to vote for Stevey. I could see myself working with him in the future; he is a loyal guy. Instead, I now wanted to cast away Fraser. To me, Fraser offered literally zero utility in a political and game sense. Fraser had already chosen to do nothing to protect his closest ally, Mimi, and in my opinion had attached himself as a yes man to the alpha males. This would be the perfect opportunity to remove Fraser from the game, before the pressure heated up at tribe swap and merge.

On top of that, I decided to run a false-flag operation with Simon's 'idol'. Stevey was working with Simon out of loyalty and loyalty alone. I predicted that Simon would not save Stevey, but I needed to create the circumstances where the pressure was real and genuine. Simon had been throwing Stevey's name around, and Fraser and Jordie had also agreed to vote for Stevey when it became clear Simon would win immunity, so this scheme was already working in my favour. If my plan was for Simon to burn Stevey, every single person in the room needed to feel like Stevey was going home, *especially* Stevey.

The added benefit for me, if I could get the timing right, would be to destroy the relationship between Simon and Jordie, ensuring that when I walked back into camp that night, it would be my alliance of three, with Stevey in my pocket and Simon never being able to work with Jordie again. I decided that I would detonate this bomb between the alpha boys after the votes had been cast, but before they were read, to ensure that Jordie and Fraser could not shift their votes onto either Shonee or Liz.

For me to pull off my plan, I had to have Shonee and Liz on board. You are strictly forbidden from speaking to other players as you are walking on camera back into the tribal council setting, so I would need to find the appropriate moment to explain my new idea to the Spice Girls.

It wasn't the only piece of delicate timing I had to navigate. For my plan to work, many things had to be executed correctly, and at the right time.

Priority number one was to forever burn the relationship between Stevey and Simon. To defeat your enemy, you have to understand them. And if there is one thing that I understood about my *Survivor* frenemy Simon, it's that he would never, under any circumstances, risk his standing in the game of *Survivor* to help somebody else if it meant he might be voted off (especially for the second time before merge).

And that's what I did. As the tribal council started, Simon pulled away with just the other men, as usual, which enabled me to set the ball in motion with Shonee and Liz. They needed a bit of convincing, so I said to them, 'I'm going to start World War III between the boys.' Shonee and Liz were happy to vote for Fraser, and the train left the station.

When JLP asked me if I was worried the voting plan might have changed, I told the truth and said that Simon told me the plan was voting out Stevey. A clearly nervous Stevey said this plan was news to him. Simon was suddenly on the backfoot, which is exactly where I wanted him.

PEOPLE CRACK UNDER PRESSURE. WHEN PEOPLE ARE STRESSED, IT EXPOSES THEIR TRUE COLOURS.

The focus of the tribal council had shifted. I had set up the framework in Stevey's mind that Simon regularly speaks to others about voting him out. I needed to keep the focus of the conversation on loyalty, because this would be the only way to make Stevey feel burned if Simon didn't save him with his idol. It would also have maximum impact when I would drop the grenade about Jordie's betrayal of Simon later in the night.

We went to vote. As Stevey was casting the final ballot, I whipped out my idol and flung it around my head. (Nothing would stop me from having a bit of dramatic fun during the best-ever tribal.)

'Wow, they're green this year, Jonathan. Isn't that interesting? It suits the colour of my dog shirt,' I announced, putting it around my neck. I will never forget the look of shock on Simon's face when he asked me what I was going to do.

'Oh, Georgie ...' said Simon with a nervous laugh, realising the game had just changed, big time. 'So ... who are you sending home?'

I fixed him with an intense stare. We were sat right next to each other, virtually shoulder to shoulder, so there was no hiding.

'Are you going to save Stevey with your idol, Simon?' I responded casually. 'Pressure's on — are you a hero or a villain?'

Simon tried to mask his shock but looked utterly baffled. How did I know about the cookie idol? It was time to let out the truth bombs about Jordie. I said that Jordie had told every single person here about Simon's idol.

Simon asked Jordie if he had any response to my allegations. Jordie had no wiggle room, so he immediately folded. That was a win for me – I thought he'd at least put up a bit of a fight. Jordie started digging up, but he only kept digging a bigger grave between himself and Simon.

'They were all coming for you, man,' he stammered. 'I was outnumbered. I had to make a call, man. I'm so sorry, man.' He also indicated that he and Fraser indeed planned to vote for Stevey. Perfection. That seed planted, I switched back to Simon.

'This is good for one tribal council,' I said, gesturing to my idol. 'And if you don't save Stevey tonight, talking about loyalty, you will literally stand for nothing.'

The rest of the tribe stayed silent.

'I will make you a deal because this is what I do, Simon. I'm begging you. Please save Stevey. Please start this new third of the game as a hero, not as a villain. Because all of these people have voted for Stevey,' I said, gesturing at the rest of the tribe. 'And that's my pitch to you … publicly.'

I rose to play my idol for myself, encouraging Simon to 'do the right thing' and save Stevey. Every word that came out of my mouth had to set up Simon to do what I thought he would do: betray Stevey's trust. While all of this was happening, it was as if Stevey was looking at the grim reaper right in front of him. Stevey had just received confirmation that he had received votes, all of them in his mind, and this kind of life-or-death moment is exactly what I needed. Stevey had to beg for his life. And he *begged*. Stevey explained what was unfolding before us to Simon.

'[George] has got us all. He's got us covered from all angles,' he pleaded to Simon. 'Save my life.'

As this dramatic moment was unfolding in real time, I now felt certain that Simon would not save Stevey as the pressure mounted. Stevey looked crestfallen, and I was adding fuel to the fire.

'You're a good man, and I really wanted to wake up tomorrow with you,' I said with a dramatic sigh. 'At least now you know who was loyal to you in the game or not.'

Before the votes were finally read, Simon said what he thought were his goodbyes to Stevey. There was a thank you – and an apology for not saving him. 'It saddens me from the bottom of my heart.'

IT WAS THE FINAL NAIL IN STEVEY'S COFFIN, AND SIMON DID ALL THE HAMMERING.

People always wonder what my plan would have been had Simon played an idol for Stevey. Now, with hindsight, we know that it wasn't a real idol, but I did not know that at the time. In this hypothetical, Stevey would have seen that Jordie had voted for him with Fraser. Fraser would still have had his torch snuffed, but I would've still walked back into camp having exposed Jordie's betrayal. This would've left Jordie completely alone and isolated in the Villains tribe as the next target of Simon, Stevey and myself. Not a bad back up.

Jonathan LaPaglia, to his credit, let all of these interchanges happen in the most organic way possible. He showed why he is one of the best hosts in the business, enabling the players to dictate the game, and he was relishing every moment of it. This was raw, emotional and unexpected. It was a tribal that couldn't be predicted or scripted by screen writers and story producers. To me, Jonathan helped create the moment and let the players involved control the story. You could tell that he was enjoying his night at the office, his smile visible in the final edit despite the drama.

I gave my final adieu: 'I protect my people to the death, because: Glory or Death. When you wake up tomorrow morning, Stevey, you will know who you can believe.'

I turned to JLP. 'Now let's get on with it.'

He read the votes. Two for George – neither counted, thanks to the immunity necklace I'd handed in.

Two votes for Stevey. He sighed heavily, waiting for that third to be read to put him out of his misery.

And then, one vote for Fraser, who'd been merely a silent audience member to the main show at this tribal council. (If only he'd known it was to be his final minutes of screentime, he might've piped up a bit more.)

Two votes Fraser.

'George, what's happening?' asked Stevey.

JLP reached into the urn and pulled out the last vote. Fraser.

'Checkmate. This was a test,' I announced, turning first to Stevey. 'Now you know who you can trust at camp tomorrow.'

Stevey is an honourable and humble man. I could see him nodding in approval. This was very, very good for me.

Simon all but ignored Fraser during his final seconds on *Survivor*, instead racing to Stevey to immediately try to repair some of the damage he'd just done. He pulled Stevey in for a hug while complaining that the nasty, conniving George had 'pulled the wool over his eyes'.

Stevey wouldn't even look at him as he uttered possibly the harshest words that have ever come out of his sweet, lovable, wouldn't-hurt-a-fly mouth: 'It's obvious that we're not friends.'

Time to twist the knife.

'Enjoy being in a minority, Simon,' I said. 'And thank you for telling Stevey he's not worth saving.'

JLP snuffed Fraser's torch, and Fraser said the first word he'd said all tribal council:

'Crazy.'

I hit my intended target and had pulled off the impossible. In one night I solidified my relationship with my two closest allies, Liz and Shonee; permanently severed any connections between Stevey and Simon, between Stevey and Jordie and between Jordie and Simon; and I removed Fraser from the game, a person who was of zero value to me politically. This all happened because I had simply made the friends I needed and then manipulated the situation to work for them – and most importantly, me.

I was able to do this because of what you have read in this book: confidence, self-belief, loyalty to my people, identifying what my allies wanted (and giving it to them), dirt digging, backing my judgement, bluff and bluster, and predicting what my enemies would do to use that against them. I out-thought every single opponent of mine with well-placed threats and created a winning scenario irrespective of the unknown outcome. I moved the odds in my favour by applying pressure, while at the same time giving my friends and rivals an option to move forward with me based on what *they* wanted, not just what I wanted. This just happened to put me in a much better position after the tribal council, in complete control of the tribe and game, rather than me taking the safe option of doing nothing. It was a glory or death moment, and history will remember it as being truly glorious.

My hope for you after reading this book is that you'll be able to apply my tips and tricks to enable your own crowning moment of glory. To win friends you have to do many things, none more so than identifying and gathering your legion of devoted followers. You do this by believing in yourself and your instincts, because if you believe in yourself, others will too. Once you have your team of loyal allies, and you do your good deeds that are beneficial for both of you, you'll have the tools needed to succeed at whatever you're planning.

To manipulate your friends, there are many different paths that you can take depending on the cards that you have been dealt.

Firstly, use any kind of criticism as an opportunity to reflect on whether you have thought of every angle to solve the problem at hand.

IT WAS A GLORY OR DEATH MOMENT, AND HISTORY WILL REMEMBER IT AS BEING TRULY GLORIOUS.

Look for a situation where you can incentivise a joint-win situation, but when it is time to pull out the stick, don't be afraid to swing it.

Don't be scared to bluff and bluster your way through a tricky situation. If you don't have all the information available to you, get it, or guess it, to test and adjust on the fly. Try to bend the rules so they work for you. If you do all of this, you can skew the odds in your favour to truly manipulate the situation for your benefit.

And when you are on a roll, just keep fishing where the fish are. Celebrate your wins and be proud of your achievements. Self-reflection is just as important as self-evaluation, because once you have achieved your glorious coronation, it is time to reset and start again.

Keep making friends, keep manipulating people, and keep winning at life. Glory!

ACKNOWLEDGMENTS

Sometimes good things happen when you least expect it. This book is one of them.

One afternoon when I was responding to my Instagram messages, in slid Georgia Frances King, my publisher, asking if I had ever considered writing a book.

I had!

I was also intrigued by her leading line: 'Hi King George, I'm Georgia King.' A few phone calls and coffee meet-ups in Bankstown later, an idea over a DM had turned into this fantastic opportunity to work with HarperCollins Australia to release my first book.

I want to sincerely thank each and every person at HarperCollins who supported me as a first-time author to bring this book to life. My stellar PR and marketing duo, Stuart Henshall and Kate Butler; the design team, who pivoted with me to create a stand-out cover that rivals the best communist propaganda posters; my editor Shannon Kelly, who guided the manuscript through its final delicate stages; and all of the sales staff who spruiked me and got into the weeds of *Survivor* strategy with booksellers around the country. I want to give a special thank you to Nick Bond, the entertainment editor of News.com.au, who pulled stories out of my mind's depths and helped me lay down the first draft. Your help was invaluable – a sincere thanks. I am grateful to have been supported by a great group who were able to create this book in what we all thought was an *impossible* timeline; I definitely would not have been able to do this without the whole team's unwavering support and guidance.

I also want to thank the large number of people who work in the Australian television industry who took a chance on an unknown boy from Bankstown and unlikely candidate for a TV show. Being able to work on Network 10's staples of programming such as *Survivor, The Amazing Race, Talking Tribal* and *Dogs Behaving (Very) Badly* has changed my life in ways I could never imagine just a few years ago. Thank you to the executive team at 10, and every single 10 staff member who I have engaged with, for always believing in me and providing me with the opportunities to live my best life. I have also had the pleasure of working with truly world-class production crew at Endemol Shine Australia and Eureka Productions: thank you to every producer, crew member, cammo, boom guy and everybody in between. It's been so much fun.